EARTH
SPIRITUALITY

Jesus at the Centre

for Lucia –

Edward P Echlin

Osterley

2003

EARTH
SPIRITUALITY
Jesus at the Centre

Edward P. Echlin

ARTHUR JAMES
JOHN HUNT PUBLISHING
NEW ALRESFORD
1999

First published in Great Britain in 1999 by

ARTHUR JAMES
an imprint of
JOHN HUNT PUBLISHING
46a West Street, New Alresford, Hants so24 9au
United Kingdom

Reprinted in 2002

ISBN 1 85608 445 0

Typeset in Monotype Bulmer by
Strathmore Publishing Services, London EC1

Printed and bound in Great Britain by
Biddles Ltd, Guildford and Kings Lynn

Contents

Preface

This book is about the earth. It is not a scientific book, nor (I hope) is it too theological for the general reader. Every author has to write from the soil on which he stands, where his life's journey has grounded him. I have been a lover of the soil almost as long as I have been on earth. I suppose I could be called an environmentalist, but certainly an earthling. My journey has also taken me into spiritual soil. I believe care for the earth and spirituality connect. We cannot do one very well without the other. So this book is about an earth spirituality and, since I am an ecological theologian, or as some say, a geologian, it includes earth theology. I have written it for all who recognize Holy Mystery grounding the earth community. Rarely a month passes that I do not receive enquiries from students engaged in eco-religion. This book is for them, for the general reader, and for all who care about God's earth. I hope it will be useful also to religious leaders and teachers among whom I have moved for much of my life.

A reader generally reads a book from the beginning. An author – or at least I in my books and articles – writes the other way around. Some readers may wish to read in an alternate way. For this book is like a sandwich: the introduction and conclusion are more crusty and practical than the infilling. Some may wish to read introduction and conclusion before turning to chapters two to eight which are more earth theological. One of the delights of being a reader, not writer, of a book is that the reader puts the last word where she or he wants it.

Some readers will find the book rather different from other spiritual earth books. I am convinced that we need not go beyond our tradition, nor parallel to our tradition, nor into any New Age inventions, to find an earth spirituality for our millennial moment. We will find what we seek in the very depths of our living tradition. We need to discover anew our own green heritage,

> What you have as heritage,
> Take now as task;
> For thus you will make it your own.
>
> – GOETHE, *Faust*

I find Jesus Christ, Christology, Christian talk and action central to *Christian* ecology. I am indebted to the ecological imagery and wonder of the Jewish Scriptures which were familiar to Jesus and the first Jewish Christians and are familiar to other faiths today. With the early Christians I ground ecology in the Jewish Jesus who mysteriously, as God and man, is both creator and earthling and, as risen, is the beginning of our future. There was in the Jewish Scriptures and their tributaries a cosmological theme of the inclusion of heaven and earth. In Jesus, God enters not only humanity but the whole earth community. Jesus includes and reconciles 'all things whether on earth or in heaven', as Paul wrote. This book is about a spirituality centred in Jesus of the earth.

The most pleasant part of producing a book is that of expressing thanks. I am indebted to many more people than I can mention here, including those to whom I have lectured in classes and conferences in North America, Ireland and the UK. Their contributions are included in these pages. Among individuals I first must mention Revd Dr Dermot Lane,

President of Mater Dei Institute, Dublin, whose persistent and characteristic prodding induced me to put these thoughts into book form. I should also mention John Seymour, premier sage of self sufficiency, whose wisdom and gentle encouragement have enlightened me over the years giving fresh insights both into the beauty of the earth and into the faith we share. I am also grateful to Dr Geoffrey Turner, Head of Theology at the University College of Trinity and All Saints, Leeds, in whose department I am honoured to be an Honorary Research Fellow in Theology. I would also like to thank Professor Charlie Moule who long ago directed me to humanity as vice-gerent in God's garden and who in recent years, in word and in script, even at ninety, has been a friend and wise critic of my work in the Sussex vineyard where we both labour. I am grateful to Robert Van de Weyer whose earth spirituality writing and editing I have long appreciated and whose expertise is responsible for the presentation of this book. I wish to thank Rolf Killingbeck, Peter King, Elizabeth Ewen and Leo Walmesley for reading the manuscript. I conclude with gratitude to three women of the earth and church who have taught me much: Sr. Ancilla Dent, of Minster Abbey, Kent; Dr Mary Grey, Scholar in Residence at Sarum College; and especially Barbara Echlin whose wisdom is in the better angels of every page. Any deficiencies are my own. I dedicate this book to my sister Martha Condit whose example and whose sons make my mother's presence tangible on the earth.

EDWARD P. ECHLIN
Bexhill-on-Sea, Sussex, 1999

CHAPTER ONE

Where I Come From

I was born and grew up in northwest Detroit, in southern Michigan, during the great depression and war, in an ecumenically mixed, indeed interreligious neighbourhood within reach of the Michigan countryside and lakes. My neighbourhood included many Jewish families, some of whom kept the Orthodox Sabbath. Jews, Protestants, and Catholics played together, but rarely worshipped together. When on rare and special occasions Catholic boys attended another church we remained silent during prayers. We never attended the Jewish synagogues or temples, nor did our Jewish friends worship in our churches. In the main I moved and learned, grew and worshipped in Irish Catholic circles. What morality and theology I learned as a boy was confident and rather legalistic, tempered by Marian and eucharistic piety, and with little room for grey. During the depression and war years the Irish Catholic community's assurance seemed indomitable. On St Patrick's Day the beer, if not the stout, at 'Tommy Long's Cafe', flowed green.

Michigan, promoted by tourist boards as a 'water wonderland', nestles like a mitten in the midst of the Great Lakes. The two Michigan peninsulas, lower and 'the upper', include countless inland lakes and tributary streams. Not far beyond my leafy neighbourhood, with its schools, playing fields and churches, within bicycle reach when we got 'two wheelers', was the beginning of the countryside, rich with rivers and lakes, woods and orchards, fertile fields and abundant wildlife. Apple blossom was the state flower. Michigan had been a state for only a hundred years. The native Americans, mostly Ottawa, Potawatomi, Huron and Chippewa, who had once flourished along the waters and in the woods were dispersed or confined to a few dreary reservations. The trappers and especially lumberjacks had felled the forests which were home and temple to the native Americans. The settlers felled their indigenous cultures. When my grandfather removed a stump on his farm he found a few finely chiselled arrow heads and an eighteenth-century musket beneath the roots. The wood of the musket butt and of the primer was rotted, only the flint of the arrows and the rusted iron of the musket remained, like the ghosts of the natives and the ashes of their campfires. There were stumps everywhere, some as tall as a boy, because the lumberjacks, working on snowshoes, wielded two-man saws even in the snow. Snow smothered the ground in Michigan from November to March, and even later in the north woods. The lumberjacks either worked during that white reality or went without sausage and pancakes for much of the year. So they sawed and chopped in the snow just as we, decades later, trudged through the slush to school.

Family farms replaced the felled woods. As I grew up, homes for car workers were replacing the cleared farms which had replaced the woods. But there were still 'swales', or small woods, of second growth trees with wild grapes and woodcock and muskrat. With good reason my father would awaken me on winter mornings with the dreaded refrain, 'Rise and shine! It's daylight in the cedar swamps.' Michigan was a blessed state, a paradise in which to grow up, and accurately called the 'water wonderland'. Summers were special. School holidays were long and leisurely. At first we spent summers in a cottage near Detroit on Lake Huron. I remember drawing water from the well, picking wild brambles, and walking along tracks with my grandmother at evening listening to the crickets and the whip-poorwill. Later my parents rented a cottage across the Detroit River on Lake Erie in southern Ontario near a town called Leamington. Only years later as a doctoral student in England would I discover the spa that gave the Ontario town its name. In Ontario I experienced the romance of fireflies and freighters at night while listening to the crickets and the owls. Even struggling farm workers were able to enjoy, free of charge, the sights and sounds of that outdoors. At that time I also learned about river and lake fishing. Few questioned hunting and fishing before the war. In fact conservationists were often field sports' keenest participants.

Above all I learned at Leamington about the lush Ontario fields with their short, intense, amazing growing season, and the incredible August harvests. The main crops near our cottage were grain, sweet corn and tomatoes grown both under glass and outdoors. Along the country roads in August as boys we followed the wagons, many horse drawn, piled high with ripe tomatoes, heading towards the large Heinz factory in town. We used to wash our faces playfully in the large beefy tomatoes fallen from the wagons. And we threw them at each other in mock 'tomato fights', like snowball fights in winter. I once toured the Heinz plant with my parents and sisters. I remember gazing into huge stainless steel vats brimming with boiling cat-sup [ketchup], like lakes of blood smelling of herbs and chilli.

At the end of the tour we were each given a small plastic pickle with 57 printed on it. I kept that pickle for many years and still associate '57 varieties' with Leamington, enormous heaps of horse drawn tomatoes and H. J. Heinz. After the Leamington summers, in my early teens I was sent to camps in the north woods, with seminarians as counsellors. There I learned more about the north woods and lakes. We looked up to the seminarians who taught us about wildlife and about prayer and who were good at baseball. My camping years ended abruptly when an aunt died leaving three younger cousins motherless. For the next four summers my uncle and my parents rented a cottage in the high pines and sands on Higgins Lake where my two sisters and I lived as one extended family with our parents, our uncle and cousins. There was good fishing in Higgins and ghosts of the native Americans who never liked the lake because it was slow to give up its dead. There were also ghosts of elk and moose, of lynx, cougar and sturgeon. The wolverine, the Michigan symbol, was extinct. Years later when I visited Rudyard Kipling's home, Batemans, in Sussex, a guide showed me the wolverine skin on the floor of Kipling's study. I remembered then the many ghosts of my native Michigan.

What haunted me – and many youngsters – the most, along with the nearly vanished native Americans, were the feathery ghosts of the passenger pigeons. Every boy then growing up in Michigan knew about the passenger pigeons. None of us had actually *seen* one. Book pigeons don't really *live* and fly through the woods at dawn. But their ghosts troubled the Michigan psyche, probably because there were still living codgers who remembered them whistling through the sky in their millions. White breasted and gentle they filled whole woods when they nested. When settlers with shotguns reached the lakes the pigeons were doomed. John Muir, when a youth in neighbouring Wisconsin, said every gun was pointed at a pigeon. It seemed that their numbers were infinite, that they would last forever. Some were caught, blinded and tied to stools as a decoy. The name 'stool pigeon' lives on. But the pigeons did not. Michigan was their last nesting habitat. In 1878 one Michigan hunter shipped east three million birds. The last wild bird was seen just eighteen years later near my grandfather's farm. The last pigeon of all died in 1914 in the Cincinnati zoo. Her name was Martha. If it happened to the pigeons – and to the dodo – we wondered as boys if it could happen to other birds, to animals, to us too. The thoughts of youth are long and deep.

The teachers who contributed to my spirituality were many and varied and lasting. My parents, as my first teachers, transmitted to my two sisters and myself the faith which their own immediate ancestors had transmitted to them. Both parents had free church tributaries in their Irish Catholic tradition. A paternal ancestor, Robert Echlin, was Archbishop of Armagh under James I, but recent ancestors converted to Catholicism before leaving the Irish midlands and the Pale last century. My own parents, born in Detroit, settled in Gesu, a Jesuit parish near the University of Detroit in northwest Detroit. There I was taught the basics of the faith by Jesuit priests and in primary school by Immaculate Heart of Mary nuns. From fourteen to eighteen I attended the University of Detroit Jesuit High School for boys. The Jesuit priests and scholastics (student Jesuits) complemented and deepened the education I had received from parents and pastors, from the Sisters at Gesu School, and from the woods and waters and wildlife of Michigan. As boys we looked up to the Jesuits, especially the young scholastics only about ten years older than ourselves. We admired their history, not only the heroism of St Ignatius Loyola and Francis Xavier, but the travels of French Jesuits in the new world. Of Canada or 'New France' the historian Francis Parker wrote, 'Not a cape was sighted, not a bend was rounded, but a Jesuit led the way.' Of the French Jesuits among the Indians, the nineteenth-century historian of the native Americans, Lewis Henry Moyer, wrote,

> The privations and hardships endured by the Jesuit missionaries, and the zeal, the fidelity and devotion, exhibited by them, in their efforts for the conversion of the Indians, are unsurpassed in the history of Christianity. They traversed the forests of America alone and unprotected, they dwelt in the depth of the wilderness, without shelter, and almost without raiment.

In our time of appreciation of religious pluralism, we may wonder about the strategy of the Jesuits attempting to *convert* the native Americans; but we cannot doubt their uncommon concern for the *welfare* of the native Americans. As boys we admired 'blackrobes' for that concern and for their courage.

People often ask when I began to include God's earth in my spirituality and theology. The response is not difficult because I have always considered Christian life as concerned with human minorities like the Amerindians, and with all the other creatures redeemed and destined for God's future. In retrospect I think the major influences were my father and two maternal uncles who were conservationists in the wilderness tradition of Henry David Thoreau, John Muir, and Aldo Leopold, the latter two being associated with Wisconsin, 'the badger state' just across Lake Michigan and very similar in climate and terrain to Michigan. What my father and uncles taught me is well summed up by John Muir. 'God's love covers all the earth as the sky covers it, and also fills it in every part. And this love has voices heard by all who have ears to hear.' Muir added that in all his close studies of wildlife he had never found an animal that was created for someone else's enjoyment and not its own. My father and uncles, like Muir and Leopold, saw no contradiction between conservation and hunting. Indeed conservation was associated with fishing and hunting in the public mind. Had they lived later in this century they may have modified their views for a smaller, more damaged, less biodiverse world. In any case when they went north hunting, into 'the thumb' of Michigan, they went to considerable inconvenience to get to Sunday Mass. I remember one October Sunday when my father handed the priest a five dollar bill after Mass, 'a fin' he called it, for abbreviating the homily 'so the hunters can get to the fields early.' There were other ambiguities with which I would later wrestle, but I was in no doubt then or now that Christian spirituality is earth-inclusive.

As schoolboys we at first found girls a puzzling nuisance and wished Gesu school were a male preserve like the private secondary schools. Somewhere around twelve or thirteen, however, we noticed that they had become interesting. Some seemed quite nice and we even thought we would like to go out with them. We didn't date much until we were sixteen. By then we were in the all boy Jesuit High School and had to date girls from mixed or all girl schools. Despite the pleasant differences, the enjoyable dates, their wit and intelligence and the humbling goodness of many girls I knew, I decided, during my final year at high school, to enter the Jesuit novitiate at Cincinnati, Ohio. It was a fateful decision. I was to remain in the Jesuits for twenty-five years. In fact I remain spiritually still a Jesuit. As the present

Jesuit General (Peter Kolvenbach) says often, there is no such thing as a former Jesuit. Once you've made the whole *Spiritual Exercises* as a Jesuit and been through the whole training you're in for the duration – which is to say, forever. Technically, or better canonically, however, I was to leave the Jesuits after twenty-five years, twelve of them as a priest theologian, to continue my work as a Catholic theologian 'in the midst' of God's pilgrim people.

The Jesuit years

In my Jesuit years I received from the Society boundlessly more than I could ever repay. God's grace mediated through the Society is as boundless and deep as the ever returning oceans. There certainly is a distinctive Jesuit spirituality. Spirituality should not be bracketed off from the rest of life but is as Ellen Leonard describes it, 'the whole of one's religious experience, including one's beliefs, relationships, and ways of acting. Spirituality is wider than either theology or morality, and can be understood as the source of both.'[1] My spirituality developed in the Society in continuity with my earlier life in a Jesuit parish and school. This is not to deny that there were radically novel influences, discoveries, and insights – for the development of spirituality like that of dogma passes through disruptive depths and shallows before continuing in newer channels. There are desolations and doubts and questions too – in a sense all of us, under God, are perpetual adolescents forever on our way to an unknown future. Sages as different as John Henry Newman and Alec Vidler have stressed the necessity of living with ambiguities: we believe with all our hearts, we sometimes doubt with all our heads. We can be at times, as Vidler said he was, sceptics in faith's clothing.

[8]

To be a Jesuit is to be formed by a little book, *The Spiritual Exercises* of Ignatius Loyola. I imbibed the *Exercises* from my first days in Ohio and throughout my Jesuit years. Certain salient insights grasped me when I was a young Jesuit, especially during two thirty day retreats in my first and fifteenth years in the Society, but also in week long annual retreats and in all my thoughts and prayers and aspirations. A preliminary note to the *Exercises* has always startled me. Ignatius says, 'it is not to know much but to savour a matter interiorly that fills and satisfies the soul.' Spirituality includes imagination. Much of our failure to grasp our own earth tradition and to attract people who care about God's earth and the future is a failure not of knowledge but of imagination. We know a lot and in an information age we have enough information. But the development of our imaginative power and our wisdom is another matter, to which I will return in later chapters. Another insight of the *Exercises* is the 'First Principle and Foundation', where Ignatius imaginatively but also dryly reflects upon the key text in Genesis 2.7 that pictures people, the *adam*, as *adamah*, an earthling of the earth. Ignatius portrays people as linked forever in a triangular relationship with God and with other creatures. People in the midst of fellow creatures, Ignatius says, are created to praise, reverence and serve God, and so reach salvation. Another – and later – exercise, a reflection upon sin, vividly portrays sin as skewing this triangular relationship. Yet despite our sins the triangular relationship continues. Ignatius tells us to thank other creatures, the angels, saints, heavenly bodies, and all soil creatures, including those that move in the waters, that, despite our sin, they support us, remain in relationships with us, and do not destroy us. Ignatius invites us to marvel at the heavens, and all the stars, and the earth with fruit and fish and

[9]

animals, and to consider how these created things speak on our
behalf in the presence of God, even when I have ignored them,
or when I have closed myself up in my refusal to praise Holy
Mystery. The daily solicitude of all these created things brings
about a colloquy (interior conversation) with the merciful God.
The meditation should remind us of what could happen today
through human technological hubris. Ignatius advises the retreatant to reflect with affection and wonder that the earth community does not create 'new hells' because of our sins,

> running through all creatures in my mind, how they
> have suffered me to live, and have preserved me in life;
> how the angels, who are the sword of the Divine Justice,
> have borne with me, and have guarded and prayed for
> me; how the saints have been interceding and praying
> for me; and the heavens, the sun, the moon, the stars
> and the elements, the fruits of the earth, the birds, the
> fishes, and the animals; and the earth, how it is it has not
> opened to swallow me up, creating new hells that I
> might suffer in them for ever.

There are in the 'Second Week', or second part, of the
Exercises many imaginative contemplations of the life of Jesus.
In the contemplations, with wonder, we gaze upon, listen,
sense, reflect, and communicate with Jesus, not as 'God striding
across the earth', but as a man within the soil community of
Palestine. Ignatius even mentions some of the soil creatures
Jesus knew on earth, with whom he was in a special relationship, including local people he knew and the animals, fish,
crops and fields of his own bioregion. I was encouraged by
Ignatius and by my Jesuit retreat directors to contemplate Jesus
in the midst of his creatures, and then to contemplate his

suffering and death, his descent into the depths, and his resurrection, again in the midst of creation. As I became more familiar with the progression of the *Exercises* I used to await eagerly
the last exercise, the 'Contemplation for Divine Love'. Some
friends said that was because I was eager for the retreat's end!
They were partly right – for retreats in those more disciplined
days were strictly silent. Even the 'thirty day retreat' was broken
only by three partial 'break days' in which we left the premises
for a few hours and walked and talked with fellow retreatants.
But I was genuinely fond of the 'Contemplation', especially the
'third point' in which the retreatant is advised,

> to consider how God works and labours for me in all
> created things on the face of the earth, that is, *habet se
> ad modum laborantis* [behaves like one that labours], as
> in the heavens, elements, plants, fruit, cattle, etc., giving
> them being, preserving them, giving them growth and
> feeling, etc., and then to reflect on myself.

I always found this consideration mind-blowing: God present
in the cosmos *as a worker*. All things, including my own gifts,
even my memory, understanding and freedom, are from him,
like rays from the sun. All things are in God, and God is in all
as a worker. Here is not deism, nor pantheism, but panen-
theism, God in all things and all things in God. No wonder
Ignatius concludes these thoughts by advising the retreatant to
reflect upon himself.

If reflection and prayer are included within spirituality, so
are informed thought and talk about God. A Jesuit thinks and
talks about God from the first day of postulancy. But he does
not initially study theology as a special discipline. I did two
years novitiate in Ohio, followed by two years of classical

studies. I studied philosophy for three years in Indiana and did 'Masters' degree work in History. This was followed by three years called regency, teaching in a Jesuit secondary school in Cleveland, Ohio. Only then, with the Jesuit training two thirds over, did I begin formal theological studies in Indiana which lasted four years, and for those who, like myself, specialised in theology six or more. I learned that theology is reflection upon and interpretation of God's Word within the living tradition of the Church; in Anselm's famous phrase, faith seeking understanding. God's Word, said Ephrem, a fourth-century deacon and poet, is like a never ending fountain: the more we drink the more we discover, the more we discover the more we leave behind for those who follow. Theology, Hans Ur von Balthasar said in our own century, is learned interpretation of God's Word – and this interpretation must be done anew for each succeeding context as history unfolds. At West Baden College in Indiana I found theological confirmation of what I had believed since I was a youngster in Detroit: God's creation and redemption in Jesus includes all that God has made and saved. Christianity may be reticently anthropocentric, but it is decidedly not anthroposolic, not about people alone. Fortunately there was a lecturer in systematic theology at West Baden, Fr. James Doyle, who realized that theology should be more inclusive than was most neoscholastic theology of the time. Fr. Doyle first called my attention to the Noah story, to the ecological riches in the Isaian literature, and to the cosmic Christ. He was at the time studying Teilhard de Chardin, who had died recently, in 1955, nearby in New York, and Bernard Lonergan, the famous Jesuit theologian at the Pontifical Gregorian University in Rome, who visited James Doyle at the college while I was there. Other American theologians, with some exceptions, tended to regard the earth as a stage upon which the real drama took place. I am forever grateful to Fr. Doyle for encouraging my interests in God's earth.

In each of my two stays at West Baden I wrote for one year a weekly column which the College provided for Indiana newspapers. During the second of my three philosophy years my column, 'Talking It Over', was directed at a general readership in about twenty papers. I received an interesting correspondence sometimes from far beyond southern Indiana. Five years later, during my first year of theology I wrote a column for young people, 'For Teens Only', a title designed to attract more than youth! That column was for the diocesan Catholic paper, but other papers also asked for copy. Once again I engaged in an interesting occasional correspondence with young readers and I received letters from adults elsewhere in North America who had read 'For Teens Only'! Writing these two columns was a pleasant discipline during academic studies. Writing for people beyond the academy and even beyond the church forced me to interpret as well as study God's Word, and I learned a lot about journalism.

From Indiana I went for a final year of reflection, or tertianship, to Decatur, Illinois and then to Ottawa, Ontario, for doctoral studies. I specialized in Anglican and Roman Catholic relations. Ecumenism was high on the agenda in those heady years of ecumenical convergence, encouraged by, among others, Pope John XXIII, Pope Paul VI, successive Archbishops of Canterbury, and scores of prophetic ecumenists and ecumenical theologians. My own theological studies took me to Oxford for doctoral and post-doctoral research on ecumenical theology especially the Anglican Eucharist. After receiving my doctorate in Ottawa and further post-doctoral studies at Union

Theological Seminary, New York, Amsterdam and Rome, I returned to Ohio where I taught for nine years in the theology department at John Carroll University, a Jesuit university with a budding tradition of ecumenical and interreligious studies, including an endowed chair for interreligious studies which enabled me to work with theologians from different universities and traditions. I also taught a night class for people who worked during the day including mothers raising young families. The Cleveland diocese put permanent deacon ordinands into my class so that they could study theology 'with the people they would serve'. That gave me the precious opportunity to work with and get to know some future deacons. With Gerard Sloyan, then at Temple University, and Richard McBrien of Notre Dame University I also addressed two national conferences of deacons and their wives and instructors. After nearly a decade at John Carroll I returned to England to lecture in ecclesiology at Ushaw College within view of the gripping 'grey Towers of Durham'. It was a privilege to be at Ushaw with its history, its link with Douai and the English martyrs, its location in the land of Cuthbert and Bede, its libraries and staff and above all, the many generous young men with whom I worked. Ushaw, like all theological colleges, was and is adapting to the changing late-twentieth-century world.

I left Ushaw – and, at least canonically, the Jesuits – to work as a theologian in the midst of the laity. I married an Anglican woman, who shared my interests in theology, ecumenism and the earth, and, in an ecumenical marriage, have lived ecumenically and happily ever after. Part of our ecumenical happiness, I should add, has included sharing our lives and homes with a pekinese. Pekes are not ordinary companions, they are the aristocrats of the canines. Pekes, with some reason, consider themselves honorary humans, or humans honorary pekes – which to a peke comes to much the same. Each peke is a furry person, an individual character, and if you like eccentric persons, you will be taken by pekes. Pekes live life at full flame, they are happy little rulers, and when, after brief lives, they depart, they leave their human companions bereft but wiser and with abiding memories. We have enjoyed four pekes: Susie, who had brown eyes, never doubted she was in charge and, when disciplined, would punish her human vicegerent with withering pouts; Joseph, a bundle of love with a black and white coat who could communicate with human toddlers; Paulinus, a northerner who never forgot he was named after the first Archbishop of York, and who objected to human women trying to tell him what to do; and Bertha, a gentle and dainty Sussex girl, happy to be named after the Queen who welcomed Augustine to Britain, and a lover of love. Pekes succeed but never replace their predecessors. Once you live with and love a peke you do so forever. When they die, pekes are best buried in their own garden where they can rule their peopled kingdom, and where you can love them forever until you rejoin them in another way of living. Hyacinths, planted as autumn bulbs, rise above the graves in early spring as the swallows return. Our garden pekes, pancosmic as we will be, rise in new life as hyacinths. Our peke is dead: long live our peke.

Much of one's platform and entrances disappear when a Jesuit theologian re-enters the midst, but as I have told other men and women altering their ministries, one reaches people in surprisingly different ways and from different directions. It is valuable for the theologian himself and for others to reach people in different modes of ministry. After my years as a Jesuit, almost 'above contradiction' in some circles, I have enjoyed and sometimes been bemused by the different receptions one receives doing ministry in the midst. Especially rewarding was a year as ecumenical lecturer at Lincoln Theological College which, like Ushaw, was – and in a continuing sense is - in radical transition. Lincoln too enjoyed the proximity of a splendid medieval cathedral. There I was privileged to teach Anglican ordinands including future women deacons and priests. There is an Anglican tradition, which includes Gilbert White and his garden at Selbourne, of integration of the natural world with spirituality. I found that tradition living among some of the mature students I met at Lincoln. As in all teaching one learns as well as teaches. I still encounter those with whom I shared 'the fellowship of the Bishop's Hostel' at Lincoln, some of whom are now in important teaching posts, for to be a deacon, priest or bishop is to teach.

Gradually I have come to realize the desirability of liberating theology from academic confinement if theology is to serve people relevantly and in practice. I have long been within, or at least in the outer court of, the cloisters of academe. Indeed while lecturing in Ohio I chaired a committee of the Catholic Theological Society of America which liaised with the National Conference of Catholic Bishops. I am suggesting the liberation not the dilution of theology. Whether in the academy or in practice good theology remains precise, accurate, disciplined and prayerful. How disengagement can take place is one of the intriguing challenges of our millennial moment. There are risks. Mistakes will be made. But, as Newman said, it is not the way to learn to swim in troubled waters never to have gone into them. How personally I have grappled with faithful disengagement I shall return to in the concluding chapter.

Trained theologians, both reformed and Catholic, were

highly regarded in the remarkable happening which was Vatican II (1962–65). In those years, and in the years immediately after the Council, theologians were regarded almost as contemporary prophets within the church. But as the Council and its optimism slipped into history, people became less interested in ecclesiology and in theologians. For people who cared deeply about the earth it became obvious, especially during and after the United Nations Stockholm Conference on the Environment, that academic theologians were not as *ecologically* prophetic as a few years before they had seemed *ecumenically* prophetic. They appeared no more prepared to provide a theologically compelling earth spirituality or to bite the sharp bullet of sustainable living, than were the political leaders and their followers described at Stockholm by Barbara Ward,

> 'Sufficient unto the day is the evil thereof' has been the law which has so far tacitly governed much of man's behaviour toward the environment. If history repeats itself in this regard, it is likely that in most places and for many years environmental quality will be subordinated to development goals.[2]

Few theologians, while they heard with their ears the prophetic words Barbara Ward was speaking, were prepared to respond to her or to Rachel Carson or to Fritz Schumacher or to other Christian environmental prophets, as they had to John XXIII. The Vatican II theological honeymoon was over. The continuing deterioration of planet earth in all its living and non-living components is the most profound challenge ever to confront the churches. The failure of church leaders to respond adequately is perhaps, as Thomas Berry has said, the greatest failure in Christian history. A principal reason for our inability to offer the earth community a genuinely helpful earth spirituality is a failure of imagination and a deficit of ecological practice in spirituality and in theology. Only at the turn of this millennium have we, God's Christian people, begun seriously to respond. This book is one small contribution to that beginning.

CHAPTER TWO

On Being Earth-Inclusive Though Millennial

The world in which I now live is very different, both ecologically and socially, from the world in which I grew up. Back in
Detroit there was a lot of consensus. Nearly everyone in my
neighbourhood – which to a youngster is almost one's *world* –
agreed on God, the desirability of worshipping him, and on the
ten commandments. Even decades later when I taught at St
Ignatius in Cleveland and, later still, when I lectured in theology in northeast Ohio there was, or perhaps better, there
seemed to be, agreed consensus on fundamentals. One of the
more lively theological debates, for example, was whether or
not we can discover the commandments with unaided reason,
or whether revelation is necessary. But there was no disagreement about the existence of the decalogue. The fact was, of
course, that the Churches, certainly my own Church, kept
doors and windows tightly closed. There were storms outside.
Suddenly when I was beginning formal theological studies a
great and well travelled man came along, Pope John XXIII,
who knew that there were fundamental debates raging, that
pluralism was on the gallop, and that if Catholics did not get
involved we would be trampled, or even worse, passed by like
sheep on the verge of life's path. As a historian Pope John knew

that our aloofness was not good for the world outside either. And so he opened the doors and windows which, as he knew, soon would have blown asunder anyway – and I found myself a young theologian in a pluralist millennial world.

Pluralism persists and with it, especially in the affluent north, an individualism that threatens not only justice and peace among people at home and abroad but life on earth. To put this another way, the rampant individualism of our pluralist millennial world brings with its fragmentation a dangerous side effect: it could, and numerous earth scientists say that it will, destroy life on earth. There lingers a famous, never convincingly disowned phrase that 'there is no such thing as society'. On a wider, more global, field there are 'justice and peace' professionals who argue that justice for human society excludes the integral earth society. They repudiate, at least for their own ministries, the third dimension of the World Council of Churches' 'justice, peace and the integrity of creation'. With such repudiation, by people who should know better, of part of earth society, it is not surprising that voluntary services are in trouble. Admirable groups who serve without monetary 'pay' find it daunting to persuade individuals to serve on committees. Some wonderful organizations even fold. Environmental NGOs (non-government organizations) frequently consist largely of white, middle-aged joiners with only a sprinkling of young people willing and able to serve without salaries and even fewer of what Americans call woopies, well-off older people. Instead of community service, including service of the whole earth community, there is individual indulgence in holidays, shopping, 'doing well', living unsustainably without regard for the future, and, in a word, looking out for one's self and perhaps some kin. The galloping pluralism to which Pope John XXIII responded has become fragmentation.

Different descriptions are suggested for our individualist and fragmented context, including post-modern individualism, economism, an increasingly competitive world, utopian capitalism and liberal democratic culture. 'I am a millennial person' means to some people that every man is an island, responsible to his own interests, making his own meaning. The Irish theologian Gabriel Daly comments,

> The post-modern age is sceptical about all truth claims, all attempts to give universal meaning to the world we live in. Today there is a tendency to distrust all institutions as controlling or manipulative. We find it difficult to see one centre in our world. Instead we see lots of different centres, each jealous of its own autonomy and resentful of any attempt by outsiders to impose their own standards upon them.[1]

In other words the unifying centre of universal meaning with which I grew up is no longer unifying. Not all accept the claims of Holy Mystery, awesome and compelling, in the depths and beyond all that exists. Even core doctrines and first principles such as 'good must be done, evil avoided', and that lying is wrong, are now questioned. God is missing but not missed. Such is our context, a challenging one in which to work as an ecological theologian. It challenges all believers who think theologically and who seek an earth spirituality. There is confusion, even among believers, about what theology, let alone eco-theology, is, and who the theologians are. I have been bemused when Christians, often from an evangelical background, in the green movement with little or no theological training say they are 'theologians', and that they can lecture on 'theology'. I am more bemused when commissioned readers or ministers say that because God has 'called' them to ministry and that they have attended a few theology courses, there is no longer need for them to read or study theology. Even the word 'theology' is differently applied as, for example, when Europhile politicians describe 'the theology of Europe'. With good reason the Jesuit theologian Walter Kaspar says, 'It is unfortunately not a redundancy to say that, especially today, a theological theology is the need of the hour.'[2]

Do-it-yourself culture

Before the windows opened I moved in a world where most people respected experience even in something as personal as spirituality, just as in the desert ascetics sought experienced persons as spiritual directors. In my Jesuit years every man had a spiritual advisor whom he met at regular intervals and at times of special challenges. During retreats we had 'directors', sometimes one for a group with similar needs, and sometimes individual directors for a 'directed' retreat. Today, however, there is less *perceived* need for 'direction'. Our present phase of individualism could perhaps be described as a spiritual do-it-yourself culture wherein for many people, God, faith, spirituality, morality and ethics, responsibility for other persons, for the earth and the future, are pretty much what each individual says they are. Sleeping around, for example, or concreting one's garden, or driving to work in congested towns, providing one's health is safeguarded, are acceptable for a millennial person. Appreciation of expertise in spiritual, theological, moral, and ecological science is suspended. For some, religion has become, as Cambridge's Don Cupitt would have it, something we ourselves construct, limited to our measurable world of experience, wholly our own construct. Pick and mix eclecticism, with a dash of one's own ingredients, for a spiritual Round-Up-Ready, is now quite common. Far from being an age in which there are no narratives, ours is an age in which there are many stories and many millennial tellers. A variety of beliefs tossed in the air like jugglers' balls challenges anyone who thinks (as I do) that Jesus has something to offer the earth community in an individualistic post-Rio age. From our origins in the burning east, we Christians have been sent to herald *good news* about God and people and the whole earth community and the union of God and humanity in Jesus. For God to become *man*, the Word become *flesh*, for Jesus to be *incarnate,* means that in Jesus God is an earthling 'like unto us' in his humanity. Jesus is God *and man*, therefore he is within the earth community, interconnected, as we are, with the whole universe, able 'to reconcile to himself all things, whether on earth or in heaven' (Col. 1.20). Christian earth spirituality is not the only earth spirituality on offer. But I insist with confidence, to Christians as well as to other believers and to humanists, that a Christian earth spirituality *does* make a useful, indeed priceless, contribution to the earth community now and in the future.

A bracing challenge

Contemporary fragmentation and earth exclusive individualism is less a warrant for anxiety than a challenge to re-engage with the depths of our own living tradition, to reinterpret and faithfully innovate, to tell people about the unique healing of the earth in Jesus interpreted for our millennial context. We need to listen to our own tradition. In the words of Benedict, let us 'listen carefully with the ears of the heart'. There is beneath individualism, economism and consumerism a void, a vacuum, a hollowness to which we can respond with the earth Jesus and

[23]

with our healing practice because we are his disciples. The challenge varies in different bioregions. North of the deforested Sahara, for example, African Christians live amid a sometimes militant, but also fragmented, Islam, which prohibits evangelization: to say – and live out – what God has done for people and the earth in Jesus, to do Christian ecology, could be life threatening. In affluent Europe, Christians – and all believers – face another challenge in metrocentre cultures which liberally permit evangelization, especially if it legitimates individual consumer and utopian capitalism, while disregarding the earth-inclusiveness of Jesus and his invitation to sustainable sharing. Not surprisingly, in aspirant Africa, in Asia and in consumerist Europe the health of the whole earth community, not excluding people, is in decline. Of Mindanao where for twelve years he worked with the Tiboli people, Irish Columban missionary Sean McDonagh writes,

> The saga of death that follows in the wake of forest destruction goes beyond the extinction of species. It also includes the loss of fertile topsoil. In the mid-1980s the Bureau of Soil in the Philippines estimated that the equivalent of 100,000 hectares of soil, one metre thick, was lost each year in the Philippines. This dramatically reduces the prospect for sustainable agriculture in the future in a country where the human population is continuing to increase.[3]

Whether in Asia, in Sahara situations or in metrocentres, Christians who share McDonagh's 'passion for the earth' are benignly marginalized, sometimes by fellow Christians. I suspect marginalization of Christian ecology, at least in the near future, will continue. But the distinctive value of the Christian contribution remains. So does the imperative to tell the world, in word *and action*, what God has done for people and the earth in Jesus. Silence in word and practice, faint heartedness because of our marginalization, is unworthy of followers of the earth Jesus. Diffidence gives the impression that we have little in our earth tradition, our sacramental heritage, to offer. We need to go forth with the high spirit of the warrior, to evangelize the shopping centres while listening to *and learning* from other stories. Michael Barnes has said often and well that we need to listen to those other stories while remaining faithful to our own. Fidelity to a tradition, telling people about God's reconciling of the earth community in Jesus, proceeds in dialogue, learning from other stories while sharing what is most pertinent *for today* in our own tradition.

In our age of individualism, where earth-inclusive Christians are marginalized, we need deeper understanding, *fides quaerens intellectum*, of where we stand as Christians in our pluralist world. We need more agreement among ourselves about God as Trinity, about the inclusion of the whole earth community in the Incarnation, about apostolicity, the earth-inclusive Eucharist and rites of passage, and the awaited new heaven and earth. We can deepen our understanding of our tradition, our exploration of the depths of God's Word, by post-critical reading of the Bible. Alone, or in small groups, preferably with a trained person or at least a reliable commentary, through *meditative reading* of the Bible we discover the unsuspected depths of our heritage.

By 'post-critical' reading and meditation I am not suggesting that we burn all bridges to recent biblical criticism (or specialized study of the Bible). Rather I am urging that we approach God's Word, in and beyond the Bible, asking inclusive questions, contemplating God's Word in a more ecological and imaginative way than have most specialists. To quote St Benedict again, 'Listen carefully with the ears of the heart'. We need to re-enter our heritage with *perceptive* imagination and with wonder. We need the exegetes – who study the Bible exhaustively with critical tools – to uncover 'the literal sense' of certain passages vital for our context, what the Bible authors intended and conveyed to their own immediate hearers. We will, in our isolated age of individualism discover within the wellsprings of the Bible and the whole living tradition testimonies and clues to the *triangular* relationship that exists, between God and his people and his whole earth. Speaking recently to his own curia at Borgo Santo Spiritu in the Vatican the Jesuit General, Peter Kolvenbach, described that triangularity,

> Ignatius affirms that the bond of this triangular relationship – God, man and created things – is so intimate that there is no authentic encounter between the human person and God which is not mediated by being inserted into divinely created things, and that conversely there is no perfect involvement in the world of created things which is not the result of a discovery of God.

When God is missing but not missed, and when created things are not appreciated, human relationships are in disarray. The shoppers' mall is a lonely temple.

To rediscover the living triangularity of our deep tradition we need the company of our organic growers, conservationists, campaigners, ascetics, artists, and poets. Scholars who find difficulty relating to the earth would do well to read the Bible accompanied by believers who tend broad beans in need of defence against blackfly. Artists and poets and environmentalists perceive depths that academics often miss. Recall the words of Ignatius again, 'It is not to know much but to savour a matter interiorly that fills and satisfies the soul'. Specialists can easily miss what Pittsburgh Theological Seminary's Old Testament scholar Donald Gowan calls 'the relatively minor theme of the transformation of heaven and earth.' The hints and echoes, the deceptively minor themes we perceive through imaginative contemplation, are what we and our contemporaries need now. The living wellsprings, seen and heard and rediscovered, will help us to restore the forests and improve the lives of the world's poor, while living in sustainable sufficiency in developed worlds. But ours will not be the last word. If the 'communion of saints' means anything it means that we are in communion with others who lived, in Christ Jesus, in the past and who surround us now, and with others who will stand upon our shoulders reinterpreting *our* words, even our last words. They will perhaps learn from us. We certainly can learn earth-inclusive wisdom from fellow communicants upon whose shoulders we stand. In surprising ways we can learn especially from some who lived briefly on our earth *before* modern physical and biblical sciences.

The spirituality of Bernard of Clairvaux (d. 1153), like that of Francis of Assisi and St Ignatius, has long fascinated me. Bernard appreciated the triadic balance of St Benedict which combined personal and communal prayer with manual work, including work in the fields and woods, and with contemplative reading of the Bible and spiritual writings. It must be said that Bernard is not a cuddly saint. Women often find him less endearing than Saints Cuthbert and Bede or Pope John XXIII. Nor is Bernard among the greatest theologians. Nevertheless his refined bearing, the power of his personality, his ringing words and valiant deeds are unique in western church history in their electric magnetism. The last of the Fathers, but in eloquence certainly not unequal to the first, Bernard served God long before modern science and biblical criticism. In his contemporary cosmology Bernard's earth was, paradoxically, relatively larger and more central than our small planet circulating its medium sized star. These very differences contribute to Bernard's freshness. His words haunt and linger on like those of an Augustine, a Pascal, a Newman. Bernard discovered God both in contemplation of the Bible and in the hills and oaks and beeches of his valley. That clear valley of the Aube in Burgundy became for Bernard and for the hundreds who followed him his pathway to the New Jerusalem.

In the midst of the natural world, in the cloister, and in the fields and woods Bernard experienced the presence of God in the risen Christ. He sought and found and 'tasted' God in 'the two books' of the natural world and the Scriptures. He rejected (in vain) the developing systematic 'schools' of learning in his century. Bernard (like all of us) had personal as well as time conditioned limitations. He is no one's *whole* cup of tea. But his communion with God in the hills and fields, waters and trees, as well as in the cities to which he travelled in service of God and the Church, can inspire us even now just as he inspired men and women in his own generation. His famous words to his friend and disciple Ailred of Rievaulx 'shout' God, transcendent and immanent, experienced here within our earth community,

> What you say about your mountains and rugged rocks
> does not disconcert me at all, nor am I horrified at the
> thought of your great valleys, for now 'the mountains
> drop down sweetness, the hills flow with milk and

honey, and the valleys are filled with corn', and rocks and mountains are the pasture of the Lord's sheep. And so I think that with those tools of yours you will be able to strike something out of those rocks that you have not got by your own wits from the bookshelves of the schoolmen, and that you will have experienced some-times under the shade of a tree during the heat of mid-day what you would never have learned in the schools.[4]

The hidden sense

When we contemplate the early testimonies to Jesus we are reminded that the real Jesus of Palestine left no writings, not even a sample of his signature in a desert cave. The various con-tributors to the Bible recall and interpret his words and deeds. Which is to say they give us not scientific history but good news, the gospels are evangelization. We would distort these four short books were we to treat them as primarily history. When we contemplate the testimonies to Jesus looking for insights we will catch glimpses in the depths, in the small print, in what is hidden, between the lines, tacit and silent. Still waters run deep – and are almost silent. 'Jesus was silent' wrote Matthew in a crisp sentence describing Jesus' response to Pilate (Mt. 26.63). Origen (d. 254), the eminent third-century biblical scholar, flung that sentence at a hostile pagan Celsus to say that there is more to Christ than meets the cursory eye. A second-century Syrian bishop, Ignatius of Antioch (d. 107), also found depths of meaning in Jesus' words and silence. 'He who has made the words of Jesus really his own is able to hear his silence' (*Ephesians* 15.2). In the silent depths are the tributaries and the subsidiarily known connotations that respond to our

[29]

needs and that of the earth in need of spiritual irrigation today. In the silence we touch the earthiness of Jesus as did Thomas when he put his hand into the silent wounds. The silent depths are loaded. When I publish a book it 'gets away' from me like a small mouth black bass slipping a hook in Michigan. Years later people tell me that something I wrote moved them. Yet I had not realized, when I wrote, all that I was saying. Sometimes what people say moved them I *intended* only in the most subsidiarily known, or implicit, way. There is more within the loaded silence of the primitive preaching than even the early Christians who gave us the first writings realized. What they put into writing grows in meaning after they have disappeared. There is a 'distanciation' between them and the writings they left behind. There is an implicit *more* in the loaded silence of their preaching which glimmers into life, like that released black bass, for us with our needs for an earth spirituality now.

When the early Christians read the Jewish Scriptures in the startling light of Jesus risen they preached him interpreted for their own generations. When we read the same scriptures *and* the New Testament, we too read the Bible on this side of the resurrection. We tell people about Jesus interpreted for *our* generation. Each generation interprets Jesus for its own generation in continuity with earlier generations. Each generation, in the useful word of the late Jean Danielou, 'reinterrogates' the tradition. We make discoveries in the depths of the silence, we make explicit the implicit. Yet we do so in continuity with the intentions of the early Christians, and with our creeds, art, liturgies, spiritualities and theologies, teaching ministries and general sense of faith. The need for continuity with the real Jesus, with the early communities, and with our whole living tradition cannot be exaggerated. The American theologian John Galvin writes,

> Without some linkage in these matters between the
> Jesus of history and the later church, it would appear
> impossible to assert continuity between Jesus and the
> church or to provide any standard by which to assess
> the compatibility of subsequent historical develop-
> ments in the church with their normative origin.[5]

In principle the whole of our tradition addresses us. The
tradition is our living memory of Jesus. Through our tradition
God communicates with us today. In one of the earliest Christian writings St Paul implicitly addresses us: 'When you received the Word of God which you heard from us, you accepted
it not as the word of men but as what it really is, the Word of
God, which is at work in you believers' (1 Th. 2.13). When we
reinterrogate that 'Word' with our unique questions for our
present agenda we act on and communicate what we discover.
But our 'preaching' – in action and words – is not *just* for our
own generation any more than the Pieta was limited to Michael-
angelo's. Our interpreted discoveries will assist those who
come after us with agendas of which we barely dream. We need
not think ourselves, ecologically and spiritually, as the last generation through whom God's Word illuminates the earth community. Faithful reinterpretation, even of our own last words,
will continue!

The stones shout
Henri de Lubac, the French Jesuit theologian and cardinal, said
that when we reinterrogate our tradition for a crisis, we should
look especially to those places where the living tradition is most
intensely expressed. The living and loving memory of Jesus
flows in many ways, many devotions, writings and works of art.

Nowhere is the living memory more intensely expressed than in the words and pictures of the Bible. When we reinterrogate those words and pictures seeking earth spirituality we may discover as if for the first time, that is, we may *realize* at last, that God creates and sustains *all things* through his *Word*; and that Word is *flesh*, is *earth*, in Jesus of Nazareth. Christian ecology grounded in the living tradition is mind blowing. Our Creator, in Jesus, is an earthling. Ecology is inherent to being a disciple of Jesus.

It is important that we contemplate not only what is explicit in the Bible, and in the liturgies and devotions flowing from the Bible, but also what is implicit, such as hints about animals, in the Jewish scriptures. There are implicit allusions, hints and echoes in the gospels that are included in the good news about God's healing of ourselves and the whole earth community in Jesus. A popular gospel in liturgies and readings through the Christian centuries has been that of Matthew. At the very beginning of Matthew's gospel there are echoes and hints of earth inclusion which have become more explicit in our Christmas liturgies, our art and in our creches. The stars and the Magi remind us of another Gentile seer, a magus named Balaam who foresaw a future star and king,

> I see him, but not now;
> I behold him, but not nigh:
> a star shall come forth out of Jacob,
> and a sceptre shall rise out of Israel.
>
> – Numbers 24.17

There is another creature in the Balaam story forever associated with the infancy – and the close – of Jesus' life on earth. Balaam rode upon an articulate donkey who, seeing more in the path than the seer saw, was wiser than her owner. Already at the very beginning of a popular gospel we recall, through the chastened Balaam, that we have responsibilities and duties to our fellow creatures, and not 'rights' to exploit other sensate beings in the earth community. We can learn much when God reprimands Balaam for striking his donkey,

> Why have you struck your ass these three times? Behold, I have come forth to withstand you, because your way is perverse before me. And the ass saw me, and turned aside before me these three times. If she had not turned aside from me, surely just now I would have slain you and let her live.
>
> – Numbers 22.32–3

When we contemplate Matthew's infancy stories imaginatively we recall the Gentile Balaam, the star with its connotations of cosmic kingship, and an articulate she-ass enjoying the instinctive wisdom of animals. Matthew's infancy explicitly includes other Gentile Magi seeking Balaam's star. With the perceptive power of imagination, artists and poets – including Francis of Assisi – noticed the star and donkey of Balaam and the pack animals of the Magi.

Matthew's conclusion, near the close of Jesus' earthly life, likewise includes Gentiles: Pilate and his wife, the perceptive centurion and the guards at the tomb. Matthew also, in dramatic apocalyptic imagery, includes the cosmos. Darkness descends, the earth quakes in its depths, the rocks break open, Jesus is buried in a hillside tomb. The whole earth community, including living creatures dependent on the sun, the stones, and the earth's depths and gardens, are included in creation, incarnation and redemption. The living tradition – including

artists' depictions of that climatic ninth hour – generally interpret the darkness and the quake as judgement. But with the
creative perception of imagination may we not discover more
than dark judgement here? Certainly the cosmic quake visibly
moves the Gentile centurion (Mt. 27.54). There seems to be
more than judgement in the early darkness, trembling earth,
splitting rocks, torn veil and stranger's grave. We may wonder if
Matthew and his community left guidance for an earth spirituality, hints of cosmic inclusion, even earth compassion, at the
death of creation's king. The late premier American New Testament scholar, Raymond Brown, points in this direction,

> If the birth of Jesus was marked by a sign in the heav-
> ens (a star's rising), his death is marked by signs on the
> earth (a quake) and under the earth (tombs). His death
> brings judgement on the Temple but also the resurrec-
> tion of the saints of Israel. Human relationships to
> God have been changed, and the cosmos has been
> transformed.[6]

Matthew's gospel is associated with Syria. And the Syrian
church was close in language and imagery to Jesus and the first
Galilean Christians. Significantly, at Sardis in 170, Bishop
Melito, in a paschal homily, vividly pictures the totally human
agony of Jesus and what approaches sympathy from his earth
creatures,

> The earth was trembling ...
> The heavens feared ...
> The angel rent his clothes ...
> The Lord thundered from heaven,
> and the Most High gave a cry.

Two centuries later Deacon Ephrem (d. 373), a native Nisibin and poet teacher at Edessa, is even more explicitly earth-inclusive than Matthew and Melito. According to Ephrem the elements and rocks cry out in protest at the innocence of the Saviour,

> Because the mouth of human beings had condemned him, the voice of Creation cried out to proclaim him innocent. Men were silent, so the stones cried out.[7]

The Syrian Christians expressed Christian ecology, an earth spirituality, with intensity through their local and cultural proximity to the Galilee Jesus, to his first followers and to Matthew who may have lived in Syrian Antioch on the Orontes. Reflecting on the Old Testament in the light of Jesus crucified and risen, Melito and Ephrem affirm cosmic inclusion, and deep earth spirituality, in the inclusive death and triumph of Jesus.

Nor were the Syrian Christians alone. Far to the colder north, in the kingdom of Northumbria the home of Cuthbert and Bede, an unknown poet genius, contemplating Matthew's gospel, attributed to all creation tears at the death of Jesus the ruler,

> Clouds of darkness gathered over the corpse
> of the ruler; and shadows, black shapes
> under the clouds, swept across
> his shining splendour. All creation wept,
> wailed at the King's death.
> Christ was on the cross.
>
> – *Dream of the Cross*

Creation, incarnation and reconciliation in Jesus include the whole cosmos, the planets, light and darkness, heights and depths, living and dead, Gentile and Jew, gardens and animals. The earth community, included in Jesus' death, is also included in resurrection.

An inclusive destiny

Had Jesus after his burial in the garden tomb survived but not risen from the dead Christianity would be a less earth-inclusive religion. Our future would be less cosmic, without the companionship of our fellow creatures. But Jesus arose and was experienced by many who had known him in Galilee and Judea, as he is experienced alive by ourselves in the Bible, in other people and the whole earth community, and in 'the liturgy, life and worship of the church' (Vatican II, Constitution on Divine Revelation, 8). Jesus risen and alive in this individualistic millennial age is the initial transformation of ourselves, our bioregions – and the cosmos. In him there is hope for our planet which shares our destiny. In the words of the most ecologically sensitive Pope of recent times, John Paul II, the resurrection 'is the beginning of a new creation, the rediscovery of all creation in God, of the final destiny of all creatures.'[8] In the earth Jesus who cried out in agony on the cross and who triumphed in the midst of God's creatures we discover, in mystery, the beginning of the earth community's final destiny.

CHAPTER THREE

Lord of Olives and Apples

When I studied philosophy and history in Indiana, Teilhard de Chardin's writings were attracting attention. His thought was so refreshingly different from the then prevalent and dry neo-scholasticism that he was regarded as a prophet by some, as unorthodox by others. The Jesuit General of the time, a cautious Fleming, asked Fr. Teilhard not to publish his writings at least for a while. All this changed when I returned to Indiana for theology. Teilhard had died in New York and Pope John XXIII's windows were open. Some soon described Teilhard, like the late Cardinal John Henry Newman, as a 'missing father' of the Second Vatican Council (1962-65), present and influential in his thinking. I think that description was true. The Council radiated hope, it used evolutionary language, was respectful of the sciences, and was optimistic, possibly too much so, about human technological 'progress'.

I was interested in Teilhard's fresh insights, regarding him – as I still do – as a cosmic mystic and a prophetic, poetic genius burning to express his intuitions about a living thrusting universe, while remaining faithful to the Christian and Jesuit tradition in which he was grounded. Teilhard was in a tradition stretching back to the Pauline hymns and Maximus the

Confessor, which in neo-scholasticism was almost silent. People were, and still are, wary of his writings partly because people never know quite what to do with poetic prophets, least of all when they write hymns to the universe. Also, and incongruously, New Age people pick and choose from Teilhard making him an object of suspicion. Henri de Lubac, a younger friend and biographer of Teilhard, helped collect and wrote a foreword to a little collection of letters Teilhard wrote parents and friends from Hastings in Sussex where he studied theology as a scholastic just before the great war. I first read the letters at Ottawa when I was beginning doctoral work at Ottawa University. Little did I dream that I would live in Sussex just minutes away from Teilhard's theologate at Ore Place. I now read the letters differently from this Sussex perspective. The collection, much studied, is on reference in the Hastings library – for Teilhard described walking the very places I and other locals now walk. Teilhard, despite his sensitivity to nature, failed to foresee the damage which the motor car, just appearing when he lived in Hastings, would do, including to his beloved Hastings and Sussex itself.

Yet despite his optimism about technology, the young Teilhard realized that behind many a silver lining there moves a dark cloud. Writing to his parents in 1911 he described his distaste for hunting on the fields and cliffs where he walked and collected the fossils which, for him, spoke of *life*. 'They don't start shooting until Christmas Day so that the birds are fatter, but then it's a slaughter. The hunter follows the path the pheasants take to find their food, and at the end of the day, you can count a good hundred dead ones. It doesn't seem too attractive.' He was disturbed by the netting of songbirds on the biodiverse Fairlight cliffs. 'In the cliffs east of Hastings, bird

catchers stretch out their nets in abundance to catch the unfortunate yellow-hammers and other little birds about to cross the
water no doubt. It's pitiful.'[1] Teilhard here illustrates what I
have described as disorder in the triangular relationship between God, his human creatures, and the rest of creation. We
encounter God in and through other earth creatures which
point beyond themselves to Holy Mystery in whom we and
they live and move and exist. The natural world – what we call
'nature' – is a living community consisting of free and conscious
members, or people, in relationships with many other beings,
living and non-living, who are more than a stage for the human
phenomenon. Other earth creatures too are subjects with
needs. To devalue and abuse them is to reject God giving himself in the whole earth community. Ecological sin is the
definitively defiant rejection of God's gift of himself in his creatures, the ultimately blasphemous sin against the Holy Spirit.

Carl Jung, an experienced observer of the human psyche,
did not share Teilhard's optimism about the technological
future of man. Jung warned that human proneness to evil,
resembling what already in the thirteenth century Aquinas had
called 'the law of concupiscence', would result in grievous
future evil. In a BBC interview Jung warned,

> We need more understanding of human nature, because
> the only real danger that exists is man himself. He is the
> real danger, and we are pitifully unaware of it. We know
> nothing of man – far too little. His psyche should be
> studied, because we are the origin of all coming evil.

Teilhard and, more pessimistically, Jung, with their different
perspectives, noticed an inherited disorder in our species.
What both men, and modern environmental scientists, describe

is consistent with the Christian doctrine of original sin and the universal need for reconciliation.

The Jewish/Christian tradition, enriched by the tributary wisdoms of several ancient cultures, offers the human community in this time of ecological nemesis several stories depicting the origin and spread of cosmic crime, including stories of rebellious angels, angel marriages with human females resulting in monstrous offspring, and the fall of a king of Tyre from a mountain Eden. Especially familiar and evocative is the psychologically profound story about Adam and Eve's stumble in the garden which illuminates our crippled condition (Gen. 2.4–3.24). The Eden story appeals to the whole person moving us to fall upon our knees in repentance as we contemplate our proneness to damage relationships, our exploitation of other creatures who in reality are earthlings like ourselves. Adam and Eve's grasp at forbidden fruit is followed by Cain's fratricide of Abel, and by Lamech's casual attitude toward taking human life (Gen. 4.8, 23). Eventually there is the flood, a new beginning, and further failures. We continue to falter today.

Throughout history, certainly in this century, some people are reluctant to acknowledge our proneness to sin and our general inability to live sustainably within the restraints of our biosystems. Like the American automobile advert we like to say, 'Progress is our most important product'. As local habitats deteriorate we deny the damage industrialism does, we try to export our western 'development' through 'globalization'. There is wisdom in the observation of Leopold Kohr, 'Wherever something is wrong, something is too big'. In the late fourth and early fifth century, the monk and spiritual director Pelagius seemed to say that our moral weakness is not inherent but that we become sinners by imitating Adam's bad example.

Admittedly, we *are* influenced by the sinfulness of the culture into which we are conceived and born. We *are* conceived into societies where injustice, including the destruction of the environment of present and future people and other earth creatures, is intrinsic to the economy, the received wisdom, the transport infrastructures. We *are* born into what are called 'sinful structures', which admittedly influence us. Pelagius had a point. Nevertheless our sinful disorder is more embedded in our human nature than Pelagius seemed to think. After decades of debate Pelagius's contemporaries, gathered in a council at the port of Carthage (418), agreed that his position was too roseate, that we are sinful not through imitation of Adam but from birth. We are, in other words, sinners even before we get going, before we bump into those sinful structures which seduce or socialize us into social and environmental injustice. We are, said the bishops at Carthage, and later, in the sixteenth century at a larger council at Trent (1545–63), sinners who are 'regenerated' in Jesus. As long as we live, however, our relationships are in disarray, we need healing. As we glimpsed in the bird netters on Fairlight cliffs whose exploitation repelled Teilhard, we humans, from our origins, are congenitally prone to exploitation of the whole earth community.

The stumble into consciousness

In his mature writings Teilhard described the evolution of our species as 'hominization', a telling word implying that our arrival was not instantaneous, we are not a seven-day wonder, still less an all at once phenomenon. Fossil evidence shows a gradual arrival and expansion, very different from 'creationist' views that say God the Craftsman created women and men instantaneously near the dawn of the earth. Our arrival, however, one species among many within the earth community, was uniquely fateful for the community. For unlike the dinosaurs that preceded us and the other primates that, for a time, co-existed with us, humanity is peculiarly prone during our brief dominion to internecine warfare, to biocide on land and sea, to the taking out of whole ecosystems and at least partial self extinction.

Our complex arrival was a gradual transition into consciousness, a drift away from the relative harmony which, still guided by instinct, our primate ancestors enjoyed. This transition into consciousness, this hominization, this irreversible drift away from instinct's checks and balances, makes humans, because we are conscious, powerful and free, more prone to error and evil than any other primate or the whole primate community. 'The more consciousness a man has', said Carl Jung, 'and the more he is separated from his instincts (which at least give him an inkling of the hidden wisdom of God) the more prone he is to error.'² *This drift, or perhaps, better, this stumble away from the comparative harmony of instinctive life is what I mean by 'the fall'.* The 'fall' into freedom and consciousness is almost a fall or stumble upwards. As soon as *homo* becomes *sapiens* we need redemption. Our greed to acquire and consume, no matter what the cost to the earth, was previously restrained by nature's wisdom. As soon as we are able, we rebel against Holy Mystery within and beyond the earth, inviting us as relational beings to grow up and live sustainably under God with responsibility for our fellow creatures. The Eden story describes this stumble *in story*. Historically there was neither golden garden nor tree nor cherubim, no magic jewelled mountain, only upright ancestors in need of love and clothing, struggling, and often failing, to grow up in response to God's gift of himself and other creatures in grace.

Mutual need

Like the first humans we, who have gradually filled the earth until the blessing to fill the earth may be accomplished, retain within our bodies traces of ancestors who were less free than we. Our protein haemoglobin is remarkably similar to that of the common chimpanzee. With them and with gibbons, pigmy chimps and mountain gorillas we share a now extinct common ancestor. We no longer share their parameters of instinctive restraint – and we lack instinct's wisdom. We are prone – and have the technological capacity – to destroy redwood forests, here since before Christ, and to exterminate our nearest primate relatives. We have captured, killed, caged and experimented on other primates bringing them to the brink of biological extinction. The cruelty of United States Air Force scientists to chimpanzees, justified as 'humane experimentation', is one of the more disgraceful pages of contemporary history, here in the west in this our time. We fell the habitats of creatures nearer home as if the earth community were economic resources. We 'globalize' no matter what the cost to the earth community. Without alluding to a 'fall' Dr Jose Lutzenberger, former environment minister of Brazil, describes our human behaviour now that we are numerous and with immense technology,

> When Brazilian technocrats look at the Amazon rainforest they see only money: six hundred billion dollars of timber. Everything in the region is a resource waiting to be exploited. It is not just dumb Brazilian politicians. It is all of us. We are destroying the planet. We find it impossible to leave places untouched.

This is as good a description of our crippled plight as I have read. In the UK and Ireland valiant groups, like the Council for the Protection of Rural England and Voice of Irish Concern for the Environment, struggle to preserve dwindling habitats from our own technocrats, politicians and from 'all of us'. What we call dominion, human priestly sovereignty under God, far from being a commission to exploit, resembles organic husbandry in a garden planet belonging to Christ, Lord of olives and apples. Christian dominion, which has been described as 'co-operative letting be', learns from nature what nature does and does not do before we *do* anything to 'improve' the soil community. Christian dominion respects the natures of God's creatures, as organic gardening works with and not against nature, attuning to the sustainable symbiosis, the 'getting along together' of healthy habitats. Co-operative letting be is as different as can be from the profit driven, development dominated mindset of utopian market capitalism described by Lutzenberger, which behaves as if it knows better than nature – or that it doesn't matter – what is good for nature. To repeat Leopold Kohr again, 'When something is wrong, something is too big'. As individuals, and through our development agencies, we can best bring 'justice' to others by living locally and sustainably, by learning from the natural world, and by attuning to nature's ways and helping others to live sustainably within their habitats. We can learn from our own domestic animals and from wildlife. Shakespeare observes,

> the honey bees,
> Creatures that by a rule in nature teach
> The act of order to a peopled kingdom.
> – *Henry V* 1.2

But since we and not the chimps or bees bring disorder into this peopled, filled and subdued planet, does the earth

[44]

community really need its people? Thomas Berry asks if we are not too malignant a presence to be tolerated, a question the very asking of which moves us to contemplate our heritage more deeply and humbly. What is our place, daughters and sons of Adam, within the earth community? I have perhaps pre-empted the question by noticing that people, as God's responsible sovereigns, conduct the earth symphony of praise and thanksgiving. Other beings, however, like bees and ants in ordered array, teach us how to behave responsibly and sustainably. John Muir wrote beautifully, 'When we contemplate the whole globe as one great dewdrop, striped and dotted with continents and islands, flying through space with other stars, all singing and shining together as one, the whole universe appears as an infinite storm of beauty.' We who, having stumbled, are nevertheless God's image, are the conscious voice of that storm of beauty, co-operating with and letting be creation's praise in creatures great and small. There is music in a desert, a forest, or a fallow field. Through organic planting and sowing and letting be, and through sharing in sustainable cities, that fallow field becomes a conducted symphony.

The trilobites and ammonites and other vanished choristers we have never known, who lived here long since and are gone awhile, apparently did quite well before the arrival of our species. Yet in a real sense other creatures need us as a *sustainably living humanity* letting the earth be and, with freedom and creativity, leading the earth community in praise of Holy Mystery within and beyond the mountain spires. Other creatures depend on earth's conductors to live in a renewable way, satisfying today's needs of people *and other creatures* while securing the future for the needs *of all earth's creatures*. To limit one's idea of sustainable development and the future to humanity, as definitions of sustainable development often do, is to condemn the whole earth community to an economist future that, like a cancer cell, destroys its own life support systems. In the 1998 *World Watch Institute Report*, Lester Brown writes,

> While economic indicators such as investment, production, and trade are consistently positive, the key environmental indicators are increasingly negative. Forests are shrinking, water tables are falling, soils are eroding, wetlands are disappearing, fisheries are collapsing, rangelands are deteriorating, rivers are running dry, temperatures are rising, coral reefs are dying, and plant and animal species are disappearing.

When development or economic 'growth' is at the expense of the planet in all its life support systems, there is disarray in the triangular relationships of God, people and the earth. Whether we are assisting our immediate neighbours or those 'overseas' we need to rethink and revise the development model that has existed since the war and beguiled even aid agencies. The United Nations International Institute for Environment and Development observes, 'Increasing material affluence can also undermine quality of life by degrading the human environment and eroding social relationships. Sustainable consumption aims to promote lifestyles that place greater value on social cohesion, local traditions and non-material values.' As Christians we can make our own contributions to personal and earth healing. Living – and consuming – locally and 'sustainably' means living with what is sufficient for ourselves and for other persons and all creatures. Sustainable sufficiency needs other models than developmental growth. In Elizabeth Johnson's words,

[46]

We need to appreciate all over again that the whole universe is a sacrament, vivified by the presence of the Creator Spirit. We need to realize that its destruction is tantamount to a sacrilege. And we need to fathom that human beings are part of the mystery and magnificence of this universe, not lords of the manor, but partners with God in helping creation to grow and prosper.[3]

Christ the olive

If we contemplate the natural world as sacrament we will find nature rich with symbols for our needs. For an earth spirituality in the world of Lester Brown, Jose Lutzenberger, Leopold Kohr and the United Nations, we need to find God, and God in Christ, in more than words. We need to encounter God in the great storm of beauty which is God's earth. Woodlands, towering oaks as at Tuamgraney in Ireland, and the sequoia spires of the Pacific invite us to Holy Mystery within and beyond their magnificence. In icons, of wood or cloth or stone, the gospel in matter and in colour attracts our whole persons. Visual arts, music and poetry speak to our hearts as abstract statements rarely do, 'It is only with the heart that one sees rightly', said Antoine de Saint-Exupery through *The Little Prince*, 'what is essential is invisible to the eye.'

One living symbol from nature which speaks to me is the companionable olive tree whose gnarled roots are forever mingled with many ancient religions and especially with Jesus in youth, maturity, and death – and with his resurrection commission to us from the olive mountain to tell people what God has done in him. There are no olives in Michigan with its crisp winters. I have admired olives in California, but the olive reigns

[47]

especially supreme in Mediterranean lands among the seven 'trees' of Jesus' own biosystem, 'a land of wheat and barley, of vines and fig trees and pomegranates, a land of olive trees and honey' (Deut. 8.8). The olive also belongs to Islam. An Arab proverb celebrates that iconic tree, 'vegetable and fruit gardens are folly, while olives are king.' Mediterranean people know in their local wisdom that vegetables and fruit, and insects and stock and whole ecosystems, flourish around the olive king in fields and irrigated terraces all over the Mediterranean. A few minutes spent planting and 'watering in' a well grafted olive sapling rewards the planter and his descendants for hundreds of years. In their durability and versatile productivity olives are indeed kings in the region where Jesus lived and redeemed the olive ecosystem.

Olives have a venerable history. Bronze age settlers domesticated wild olives, planting them in hills and fields, and then terraces, throughout the Mediterranean. The tree which Jesus knew best was the European olive, a variety of the *Olea* genus. There are now in the crowded Holy Land virtually no undomesticated 'wild olives'. Where olives grow there are – or were until recently – people who planted and cared for them. Two barren trees at Har Boqer in the Negev desert and a few on Gebel Katerina in Sinai still blossom clinging to life in today's climate with its numbing desert nights when even hardened border guards wear balaclavas. Those few barren desert olives are remnant survivors of a soil community whose climate was warmer and wetter.

Windswept islands in the inmost sea, Crete in particular, illustrate in their olive plantations the symbolic possibilities of the olive for the gospel of personal and earth redemption. A weary Odysseus clung to sheltering olives in the land of the Phaiakians where 'neither the force of wet-blowing winds could penetrate, nor could the shining sun ever strike through with his rays, nor yet could the rain pass all the way through them.' Christ's own contemporary, Paul of Tarsus, compared Christians to wild olive branches grafted onto the cultivated Jewish olive tree, 'you have been cut from what is by nature a wild olive tree, and grafted, contrary to nature, into a cultivated olive tree' (Rom. 11.24). Irenaeus (d. 200) compared Christians to branches grafted into *Jesus* the symbolic olive tree. Cyril of Jerusalem (d. 386), living near the Mount of Olives, Gethsemane and Golgotha, saw in rooted olive saplings, in spring's delicate new growth, and in the living branches of recently pollarded trees, symbols of resurrection. Like Irenaeus, Cyril compared Christians to wild branches grafted into Jesus the true olive, 'You have been separated', he said, 'from the wild olive tree and grafted on the cultivated tree and given a share in the richness of the true olive.' Olive trees, some of which still grow in Gethsemane where Jesus prayed beneath the shelter of their olive ancestors, evoke memories of Jesus in his life, his last hours, and in his risen commission. Olives, like all the natural world, are iconic: through, with and in the earth community we discover Jesus crucified and risen in all his creatures. Olive oil mixed with balsam is part of Christian rites of passage, symbolically integrating Christians more deeply into the earth Jesus. Other earth creatures should be included in our worship as were oil, honey, milk, beeswax, bread, wine and water in early Roman Eucharists.

Probably the closest comparison to a European olive is the standard (or half-standard) apple in a traditional English or Irish orchard. The apple too is evocative of biodiversity and the praise of God by his creatures. The apple in a traditional orchard, as for example on the Marcle Ridge in Herefordshire, in parts of Kent, and in Kilkenny and Armagh, Ireland, not to mention the lake blessed orchards of my native Michigan, is among the most social creatures in our northern bioregion, sheltering people, domestic and wild animals, fowl, herbs, fruit, insects and vegetables, micro-organisms and mistletoe, providing kindling and logs for winter fires, a whole renewable ecosystem. Most of what we call interdependent biodiversity, such as mixed organic husbandry, catch cropping, permaculture, self sufficiency, renewability, regeneration, partial self sufficiency – all this is visible in sustainably nurtured olive fields and traditional apple orchards. The biodiversity of the olive, and in our northern climates the apple, should integrate our living of the gospel, in word and in colour, in our sacraments, our ministry to people and the earth, and in our sustainably sufficient living.

Below the olive line the olive soil community is wide and inclusive. From the community centred around that magical tree a galaxy of earth's good gifts come including manure, fodder, logs, kindling, honey and poultry. Anyone who beholds and listens to that silvery tree encounters a whole delightful, almost miraculous community, moving human beholders to gratitude. 'From each tree all kinds of varied delights', writes Deacon Ephrem, '– this too is a great wonder, as great as the miracle at Cana.'

Ephrem knew his olives. Close in time and tongue, customs and biosystem to Jesus and the first Christians, Ephrem compared disciples to silvery leaves clinging to 'Christ the Olive' through the blasts of barren winter,

> The prudent olive has no fear
>> of the cold which terrifies all
> Under the scourges of freezing winter
>> its leaves stand fast, as though faithful
> They are an image of the faithful
>> Who persevere in Christ the Olive.

In persecution the faithless have fallen like leaves
    which do not abide on other trees.
But Christians hanging on Christ
    are like olive leaves in winter
    all of them planted wholly in Him.

                                    – *Hymns on Virginity*

Conclusion

There are in Hastings Museum many of the fossils, some on permanent display, which Teilhard de Chardin collected in his Sussex years. For Teilhard, grounded in the *Spiritual Exercises* and in the Pauline testimonies to the cosmic Christ, the creatures whose fossils he found still exist. The fossils point not to a dead past but towards the living future. The whole earth, suffused with the cosmic Jesus, lives and will live and shares our future. Near the end of his life Teilhard wrote,

> All that I can remember of those days ... is the extraordinary solidity and intensity I found then in the English countryside, particularly at sunset, when the Sussex woods were charged with all that 'fossil' Life which I was then hunting for, from cliff to quarry, in the Wealden clay. There were moments indeed, when it seemed to me that a sort of universal being was about to take shape suddenly in Nature before my very eyes.[4]

I think of Teilhard a lot, especially when in winter I put out food for the song birds of Sussex a few miles from where he admired them. There are very few varieties left, so few that when a migrant appears we stop what we are doing and just watch and admire. Sometimes we alert a neighbour especially where there are children. I occasionally put a rotting apple at the stand. The birds hollow it out beautifully like a fragile green shell. Our mistreatment of our bird companions, and of the forests and fields, and, especially poignant, of our sensitive chimpanzee relatives, reflects, as in a mirror, our stumbled condition. We are sensate beings who, from our origins, stumbled, or blundered, into awesome, almost awful, freedom – and we need reconciliation which Christians find in Jesus. There are truths, like thoughts, too deep for words alone. Reconciliation in Jesus is a deep truth.

I find both light and comfort in the traditional association of Jesus with the rugged olive surrounded by living dependent creatures. Here in Teilhard's, and my own lush Sussex, the olive, or perhaps for precision I should say the olive equivalent, is the northern apple. There are over 2,300 apple varieties in the national British collection nearby at Brogdale in Kent. Each – and there are two of each! – is a small ecosystem. In fact at Brogdale the windfalls are left on the ground where microorganisms recycle them into humus which in turn rises to life in the tree. Our northern apple trees in our own gardens, and especially in biodiverse orchards of standard trees surrounded by flocks, insects, animals and family farmers, are a symbol of life through and with Christ, Lord of olives and apples.

CHAPTER FOUR

Jesus Within the Earth Community

The birds in my garden enjoy the shelter of apple trees in summer when the leaves are lush. Still more in the orchards, especially with well spaced large trees, the birds enjoy the company of the whole orchard community. In olive plantations known to Jesus there were protective leaves in all seasons. When studying the ecology of places where he lived in Palestine, I used to wonder if the local birds, animals and trees were descended from the ones he knew and who knew him. Once in Jerusalem, in a lull of peace in that torn interreligious city, I sat on the Mount of Olives in spring a few weeks before Passover. I always carried a small New Testament with me, the gospels read differently there than anywhere else on earth. I turned to Luke, 'Every day he was teaching in the temple, but at night he went out and lodged on the mount called Olivet' (Lk. 21.37). Amazingly, as if in a projected dream, I then noticed the wide variety of birds around and in the trees, and the sheep grazing beneath the trees. Ever since that spring afternoon his much quoted sayings about the birds and sheep and other wildlife have meant more to me and made him seem closer and more biodiverse.

Those creatures on the Mount and in the fields near the

places he lived were Jesus' contemporaries. He actively experienced and shared the Holy Land with them. Their successors today are especially interesting, not because they are created and saved more than we and *our* contemporaries, but because they represent the whole universe community, past, present, and future including species now extinct, visible to us, if at all, in fossils or libraries or simply pancosmic as we will be.

We cannot to our complete satisfaction reconstruct the real Jesus, with his contemporary earth community, who lived in first-century Palestine. We have no recordings, pictures, fingerprints, not even a contemporary icon. As John Meier says, the *real* Jesus of Nazareth was 'a man who died in his mid-thirties and whose first thirty-two years or so are almost completely unknown and unknowable.'[1] We can, admittedly, piece together the *historical* Jesus with the help of sensitive exegetes, archaeology, history, and the relics of Palestine flora and fauna such as the community I experienced briefly on the Mount, but the *historical* Jesus is 'not the real Jesus, but only a fragmentary hypothetical, reconstruction of him by modern means of research.'[2]

And yet we can know Jesus. To know Jesus *in his relationships* with other beings, as on the Mount and in Galilee, we reflect also on what is tacit, implicit, in the small print, and between the lines of the New Testament. Through contemplation of the Bible within the living memory of the Church we encounter not a historical reconstruction but Our Lord Jesus Christ. This is what many artists, poets, ascetics, and Christian environmentalists have done – and the Jesus they have discovered and known is not God striding across and above the earth but Jesus of Nazareth 'like unto us in all save sin', preaching an inclusive future kingdom already begun in his deeds and words. There is very little in the gospels about Jesus' Nazareth years, yet through imaginative contemplation of those years we make discoveries there. As examples of imaginative contemplation, grounded in the inclusiveness of the Bible, we notice no fewer than three meditations on the tacit, hidden Nazareth years in the *Spiritual Exercises* of Saint Ignatius Loyola. With imagination we may place ourselves in hilly Nazareth with its few hundred families and their sheep and goats, oxen, cattle and donkeys. In those green and brown and stony hills we may imaginatively observe the growing Jesus (Lk. 2.40, 52) learning, especially from his mother, about the useful elder trees, the scattered Tabor oaks and Aleppo pine, the nettle, bramble, mallow, and startling yellow chrysanthemums of April, the galaxy of weeds and herbs and wild flowers which later he compared to Solomon's attire. Grapes grow and grew in Nazareth's old town, their branches nourished by the everlasting vine. Jesus wondered at their rapid growth, their ripening in the burning sun, and their harsh winter pruning, he learned about apples, almonds and pomegranates, he saw figs swarming from rocks offering two, even three crops of dripping sweetness. When they began to put out leaves, as did the other trees, he knew that summer was here (Lk. 21.30). All this, and more, biodiversity, he, an eldest son, discovered with the assistance of his mother and extended family. The Nazareth years, like Abraham Lincoln's prairie years, were the years in which he learned about the soil. Above all he learned about the olive community, perhaps in a family field near the village, possibly on well maintained terraces clinging to denuded hills. Here in the olive groves was that astonishing biodiverse world of the psalms, prophets, Genesis and the rabbis; the whole earthly creation from bees and gnats to cisterns, manure and fodder, and families beating and pollarding trees in the lull of winter. Discoveries about

[55]

Jesus await us between the lines of the Bible, nowhere more wondrously than in these quiet, learning, supportive Nazareth years when Jesus first learned about the soil community, together with his siblings and young contemporaries, noticing the wild iris and the cyclamens, small goats and Galilee lizards and transient African hummingbirds, in the shade of the olive.

We may place ourselves at the green hills and white walls of Nazareth with Mary, when she, who as mother was a primary teacher, 'pondered' certain thoughts in her heart (Lk. 2.19, 51). Mary with whom we pray in Nazareth has yet to learn what we, on our side of the resurrection, already know: that she is God bearer, *theotokos*, that her son, human like us and learning from her, is Maker and Saviour of the olive ecosystem. Authentic Marian devotion goes with Mary to her son. We may imaginatively address her in communion with an eighth-century Celtic ascetic,

> Your son of fair fame
> owns every bird that spreads wings
> – on wood, on land, on clear water.
> He it is who gives them joy.[3]

By meditating on God's Word with ascetics and poets, artists and Christian environmentalists, we make discoveries and enjoy surprising insights which continually escape many urban exegetes and theologians. The narrative about Jesus with the Syro-Phoenician woman, for example, may be 'a composition of the early church' showing Mark's less than brilliant precision in Palestine geography – but through that touching story we are reminded that in Jesus' world small dogs played in Gentile homes, and that Jesus was aware of their behaviour (Mk. 7.28). While the story of Dives and Lazarus may belong to 'the special Lukan traditions', the story also shows that in Jesus' world small dogs roamed crowded streets and may have attended executions at Golgotha. With imagination, and with theological reserve, we may wonder if the earth community which did *not* desert Jesus at Cavalry may have been more varied than even the beloved disciple explicitly testifies (Jn. 19.25). Job and Isaiah mention dogs, as do early writers such as Tobias and Philo. These faithful animals, like swine and foxes, may to the Jews have been 'ritually unclean' – but they were around in the time of Jesus. We will never in this mortal life *know* – but with reticent imagination we may *wonder* if dogs at Calvary were possibly the first members of our earth community to drink blood from the open side of Our Redeemer (Jn. 19.34).

The Christology of Jesus

Christology, refined thought and prayer about the meaning of Jesus, began not in ancient monasteries nor cathedral schools nor even in the specially revered teaching of the early Fathers of our faith, but in the human mind and heart of Jesus. His Christology, in organic continuity with that of the apostolic communities and our own, was, I suggest, more ecologically inclusive than most Christian reflection to date has recognized. The Christology of Jesus is often in the small print, written between the lines, awaiting our imaginative discovery and healing practice. Jesus, familiar with the responsibilities of kingship, preached God's kingdom knowing he had a central place in that kingdom's coming. 'He saw himself as so important,' writes Raymond Brown, 'that rejection of him (not only God's message) would constitute the course for divine action against Jerusalem and the Temple.'[4] By foreseeing his own vindication

[57]

Jesus foresaw implicitly the transformative healing of our earth community.

By insistence on imagination, I am not suggesting that we project a post-modern Jesus, but that we incarnate our discoveries, give body to thought, that we half *create* and half *perceive*. I mean listening to the heart's reasons in a renewed appreciation of our Bible while always learning from and listening to commentaries of sensitive exegetes. I mean that *we connect*. Discoveries in the living springs of God's word are connective, stirring the eureka syndrome, one discovery leading to another. Jesus we will find is greener than we knew. The women and men who transmitted the Jesus traditions were, like ourselves, embodied and constricted *people*. They did not, indeed could not, realize all they said, nor say all they knew. Above all, neither Jesus nor the first communities asked questions about our ecological crisis which worsens daily, nor were they bemused, as we are, by the reluctant, fragmented and partial response of today's Jesus movement. How could he and they? But in the tacit depths of what they thought and said, between the lines of the four gospels, there is a surprising ecology of Jesus awaiting our discovery – and response. What Gilbert Chesterton found in the subconscious minds of authors of classical literature is no less true of the apostolic people, some of them anonymous geniuses, who proclaim to us the incarnate Jesus understood on our side of the resurrection,

> Criticism does not exist to say the things about authors that they knew themselves. It exists to say the things about them which they did not know themselves. If a critic says that the *Iliad* has a pagan rather than a Christian pity, or that it is full of pictures made by one

[58]

epithet, of course he does not mean that Homer could have said that. If Homer could have said that the critic would leave Homer to say it. The function of criticism, if it has a legitimate function at all, can only be one function – that of dealing with the subconscious part of the author's mind which only the critic can express, and not with the conscious part of the author's mind, which the author himself can express. Either criticism is no good at all (a very defensible position) or else criticism means saying about an author the very things that would have made him jump out of his boots.[5]

Visions in the air

Nazareth, where Jesus lived his formative years, is walking distance from Hellenic Sepphoris and Tiberias. Even hilly Gischala, a fertile paradise of cultivated olives and fruit, was on the route to the coast. Ideas and recurrent visions, like modern vehicular emissions, know no bypasses. As a learning young craftsman Jesus, conversing in Galilean Aramaic and, possibly, Greek and Hebrew, *learned* from older men of his time and place (Mk. 6.3; Mt. 13.55). As a maturing Jew, he listened and learned from rabbis and teachers, in synagogue, school and temple. If we presuppose that Jesus was somehow immune to the cultural, even Hellenized, air breathed in the hills, or that the first Christians were unaffected, perhaps we should reconsider our presuppositions. N. T. Wright observes, 'Any idea of a hidden curtain between Judaism and Hellenism, in the sense of a geographical line at which it might be said that the one stopped and the other began, must be completely rejected.'[6]

Within the inspired oral traditions, not all of them Jewish or

Christian, with which the literary framers of the New Testament worked, were echoes and hints that would have made the final authors or redactors of our Scriptures 'jump out of their boots'. There were dreams of human and cosmic harmony in the Hellenic air which entered the human milieu which incultur- ated Jesus. Which is to say there were stories and dreams in Jesus' times about peace between people and God's other crea- tures which would have been more or less familiar to Jesus. There was, for example, the portrayal by Virgil, in his Eclogues, published in 37 BC, of a vision of terrestrial harmony in which 'the soil will suffer hoes no more, nor vines the hook, the sturdy ploughman too will now unyoke his team'. Equally intriguing, considering the poet Horace's popularity in the time of Jesus – the Augustan era – is that poet's dream, published in 29 BC, wherein,

> tigers shall love to mate with deer,
> and the dove shall pair with the kite,
> the trustful herd fear not the tawny lion,
> and the goat, grown smooth with scales,
> shall love the briny waters of the sea.

More familiar to ourselves is the famous Isaian tripartite poem portraying peace between children and reptiles, and the similar- ity of the word *nazir*, the awaited shoot or branch, and the name of Jesus' own village, a similarity which did not go unnoticed by Matthew's community, for Matthew describes Jesus as 'a Nazarene' (Isa. 11.1–9; Mt. 2.23). There were also in the hill air dreams of a just *individual* at peace with the whole earth com- munity, dreams of agricultural fertility which could well have influenced Jesus and his parables featuring seeds and stony ground and seed-eating birds (Job 5.22–3). There are visions of ecological harmony in the New Testament itself drawn from the general milieu that moulded Jesus, his family and first disciples (Rev. 5.13; 22.1–5). The Ceasarea Philippi district was associated with the pagan fertility god Pan. In this area tributaries of the fertile Jordan are visible. If the gospels hint at some significance of the place where Jesus praises Peter near Caesarea Philippi, it seems appropriate that successors of Peter, no less than the patriarchs, like good shepherds lead their sheep in earth reconciliation. Indeed some recent popes and patriarchs and archbishops have been ahead of their brother shepherds and flocks in recognizing Christian responsibilities for all the earth, including the responsibility to eliminate militarism.

The gospel prologues

Marks's brief prologue, especially when read with the Marcan appendix, contains connotations of peace with all creation (Mk. 1.13; 16.18). Alone among the evangelists Mark, after the baptism by John, explicitly portrays Jesus with wild animals. There are more than large animals in the Judean desert where Mark and the other gospels place Jesus. The burning desert has a special biodiversity of feathery, crawling, and furry creatures, shaded by succulents holding life-giving liquid. Jesus, anointed by the Spirit and recognized as God's beloved Son is, in Mark, Jesus with the animals of the wilderness (Mk. 1.13). Although very different from the desert, the Jordan rift, in the time of Jesus, was also a wilderness, one where living creatures clustered in and about water. Ignatius, bishop of Antioch (d. 107) was among the first of many eastern writers to notice the impact of Jesus on wetlands, especially on the Jordan where he was baptized. 'He was born and was baptized in order to purify the waters by his passion' (*Ephesians* 18.2).

Matthew's prologue, as we have seen, recalls the story about an animal very different from the wild creatures of the desert and the rift. Matthew's infancy story recalls the ancient magus Balaam who thrice struck the she-donkey wiser than her human owner, 'a dumb ass spoke with human voice and restrained the prophet's madness' (2 Pet. 2.16). There is, moreover, near the close of Matthew's gospel another patiently majestic donkey in whom the poet Chesterton saw more significance than seems to have occurred to exegetes and theologians,

> Fools! for I also had my hour;
> One far fierce hour and sweet:
> There was a shout about my ears,
> And palms before my feet.
>
> – 'The Donkey'

Luke's infancy story gives us the manger which has warmed millions across the Christian centuries, especially since the thirteenth-century crib of Francis of Assisi at Grecchio. The manger in the Jewish Scriptures is often associated with the domestic ox and ass. Ascetics, artists, poets and environmentalists, most famously St Francis, have associated these animals, and sheep, with the birth of Jesus. Ignatius of Loyola, proposing an imaginative 'prologue' to a nativity contemplation draws freely on Luke's infancy,

> Think how our Lady already with child for about nine
> months, as it may piously be thought, seated on an ass,
> left Nazareth, together with St Joseph and a servant girl,
> leading an ox, in order to go to Bethlehem to pay the
> tribute which Caesar imposed on those countries.

Luke says Jesus matured at Nazareth, a member of the earth

community growing in wisdom, age and grace in the Galilean hills. The importance of this 'hidden life' is hardly new, it has long been recognized within the Christian ascetical tradition. We used to devote a whole day to the hidden years in our annual retreat. What is relatively new is our current search for ecological insights in those hidden Nazareth years. The few adult sayings of Jesus preserved by Luke, who shows more interest in Nazareth than the other gospels, echo the Nazareth influence. Jesus of Nazareth was attuned to the natural world and was uncommonly sensitive to its ways. The earth creatures who shared life with the real Jesus in Nazareth are for us representative of what John's brief prologue calls 'all things', of all time and place, of stories old and new, created and preserved in God's word and held together in Jesus (Col. 1.17). It is moving to contemplate Jesus with the representative earth community of Palestine who briefly shared with him this planet.

Jesus and feathery creatures

Palestine, with the Nile valley, is a migration corridor for numerous bird species in spring. The diversity of Jesus' time may be inferred from estimates that there are now around 400 bird species in the Holy Land, comprising residents, summer breeders, winter visitors, transient migrants, and stragglers. The diversity of climate and terrain in Palestine attracts different species. The four feathery migrants described by Jeremiah may still be seen coasting north on the April thermal winds above the Holy Land (Jer. 8.7), the white storks patiently recovering energy on fields near the coast when the winds go cool.

Jesus knew aquatic birds near the Jordan and larger scavengers at the life filled lake. He would have seen raptors patrolling the skies above fertile land with its groves, fields and vines. He observed pigeons and doves nesting in the ubiquitous Palestine rocks, where they lay eggs and feed vulnerable fledglings. Squabs are easily taken from accessible nests for food or sacrifice. His compassion for wildlife appears in the gospels when, urging his disciples to dovelike simplicity, he tempers this warning with an endorsement of reptilian wisdom. A serpent needs cunning to survive where there are large mammals present (Mt. 10.16).

People are, says Jesus, *a fortiori* precious, but wild birds (and domestic sheep) are also inherently valuable to his Father *in themselves*. In a vivid picture Jesus describes birds nesting in a mustard bush, the largest of the annual garden herbs, a brassica providing rare shade and a micro-habitat for birds and insects, yet germinating from one of the smallest seeds. Jesus knew that seed eating, feathery creatures, then as now, depended on nature's seminal prodigality (Mk. 4.8). To his Father, *each* bird is precious. He (like Teilhard de Chardin at Hastings) was familiar with the custom, still enjoyed in many Mediterranean (and other) countries, of snaring and eating small birds (Mt. 10.29–31; Lk. 12.6–7).

Some larger feathery creatures, then as now, were domesticated. Poultry had been eaten for millennia. Raucous cocks served as prototype 'alarm clocks' on camel caravans lending their name, at cockcrow, to one of the Roman watches (Mk. 14.30). Hens were quieter and more gentle than their dominant partners. Jesus compared their maternal tenderness to his own affection for Jerusalem (Mt. 23.37).

The canine presence

In the time of Jesus, wolves prowled the hills and scrub and even the pastures. Palestine wolves reach four feet in length and have tails of about fifteen inches. They whelp up to twelve pups. Wolves contemporary with Jesus were probably similar to the pale brown Syrian wolves which still prowl at dusk, furtive and suspicious, in northern Galilee near the Syrian border. Wolves prey on wild mammals and domestic sheep and goats. In the gospels they are pictured as aggressively unlike herbivore sheep (Mt. 7.15; Jn. 10.12).

Although desert foxes prowled the wilderness, the foxes to which Jesus refers in the gospels are almost certainly the Palestine red fox, relatives of European foxes, nocturnal loners about two feet long with bushy tails. Red foxes hole up in the day even in the relative cool of winter. They prey not gregariously like wolves and jackals but alone, eating fruit and vegetables as well as furry creatures and birds. When a young man asked about following him, Jesus contrasted his lifestyle with that of birds and a red fox. Birds have nests, foxes dens, but he had no fixed abode (Mt. 8.20). He likened the fox to Herod Antipas, a long-lived scion of a precarious family and a ruler of Galilee (a tetrarch) for forty-three years. A male descendant of Herod the Great needed versatile cunning to survive that long. Here in England, a European fox, resident of a nearby woodland, forages nightly in my garden, always securing escape routes through, over and under hedges. Fish bones, feathers, vegetable remnants, and, in the rare snow, canine footprints larger than my peke's, testify in the morning that he has visited. My fox, named Antipas, is a wily survivor. The Lukan metaphor still speaks.

Cloven-hoofed goats, relatives of the wild ibex clinging to survival in the crags of Crete, were sources of milk, a variety of 'cheese', leather, cloth, parchment and, especially associated with the imagery used by Jesus, wineskins (Mk. 2.22). Indeed

Bedouins used goat waterskins until the arrival of tin containers in World War II. Goats strip a hillside more thoroughly than other stock. They not only devour seedlings, crops and maquis, but like their Cretan relatives, they browse clambering *into* trees. Goats did almost terminal damage to the once biodiverse oak woodlands of Galilee and the Sharon plain. Even now I have seen them browse and damage mature olive trees when shepherds are unscrupulous and landlords absent.

Sheep symbolism pervades the Christian story. There were shepherd and sheep in Luke's nativity. Jesus was identified by the Baptist as God's lamb (Jn. 1.29, 36). Jesus expelled sheep traders from the temple court (Jn. 2.14). He was the good shepherd, his disciples like 'sheep without shepherds' (Mt. 9.36). The last supper probably included a lamb. He was, says the fourth gospel, executed when (other) lambs were being prepared for Passover (Jn. 19.14–16). While Palestine shepherds know their sheep and goats and separate them at night, the transient sojourner, by contrast, to distinguish these similar furry creatures must look closely at the tails (Mt. 25.32). The shepherd metaphor for Jesus – and for ourselves – has priestly and kingly associations. The shepherd king of the biblical *ideal* was to rule with compassion and wisdom, his justice included hills, fields and weather, in a word, soil fertility (Ps. 72.3, 6, 16). The pastoral kingly metaphor, whether for Jesus or for ourselves, does not limit one to a particular territory. But it should be said that too much import, export, foreign holiday and travel, even on 'development' missions, is unsustainable. The human presence under God, if it is to be responsible, sustainable and within the Jewish kingly ideal, will be more humble and local. There is perhaps a surplus of meaning, much for us to ponder, in W. H. Auden's profound words, 'When kings were local, people knelt.'[7]

Water creatures innumerable

As a boy in Michigan I saw the gleaming eggs or roe of many a fresh water perch or bass or sunfish. I did not realize, though it seems logical now, that the freshwater fish with its seemingly infinite roe, is an ancient fertility symbol. Seeds evoke fertility. Fish symbolism takes us back to the intimate circles of Jesus, to Jesus himself, his deeds and words, his human mind and imagination. The fish is a silvery reminder of the continuity of the imagery of the real Galilee Jesus, of the first Christians, and of the Jesus we meet in the New Testament preached to us by those who knew him near the lake on both sides of the resurrection.

The Sea of Galilee, also known as Lake Tiberias, Gennesereth, or Chinneroth, is a gleaming expanse of fresh water in a parched landscape, the whole now threatened by tasteless Israeli 'development', the lake stretching roughly 14 by 8 miles, some 112 square surface miles, and about 140 feet at its deepest. Except for large grey mullet, introduced by Israelis as fingerlings and hauled from nets by chilled fishermen at dawn, the lake community appears quite similar to what it was then. When Jesus lived, and refrigeration was unknown, sardines were dried in the sun and salted. The portable fish of the feeding traditions were probably salted sardines. There are in the lake tilapia, of the Cichlidae family, mouth breeders carrying eggs until minnows hatch swimming. Now called 'St Peter's fish', tilapia seem reasonably available in restaurants in densely populated Israel and are popular with tourists. The puzzling story about Peter looking for a coin in the fish's mouth, unique to Matthew's gospel, teaches us to avoid giving scandal, but Matthew never tells us what Peter really finds! (Mt. 17.27).

Another Matthean story, about not rewarding a boy by

giving him a snake, can be puzzling. Yet the story about the boy and the snake may imply that Jesus, from his time living on the lake, was familiar with terrapin and with water snakes which are occasionally snared by fishermen (and boys) using hook and line. Also special to Matthew is the comparison of 'the kingdom of heaven' to a drag net (whereby a fishing partner in a boat encircles an area with the far end of a net) (Mt. 13.47). Net fishing can be sustainable providing human population is in balance with a lake ecosystem and fishermen take care not to damage marine habitats and to return smaller fish to the lake. There is nothing explicit about marine conservation in the gospels, nor are Jesus and the disciples portrayed as conservationists. But the narratives imply a reasonably sustainable way of proceeding by Galilee fishermen on the lake.

John narrates a miraculous catch, followed by breakfast with the risen Jesus on the shore (Jn. 21.11–13). In a similar scene Luke implies that Jesus ate fish (Lk. 24.41–3). Luke's final seaside narrative is about the risen Lord, his close disciples, and the fish of the lake with which Jesus is forever associated.

Brother Snake

The snake, like the freshwater fish, was an ancient fertility symbol long before it became a Judaeo-Christian sign. Snake symbolism needs caution. The snake like the scorpion is often portrayed as a *symbol* of evil, frightening to humans. But in themselves reptiles, like all animal and plant creatures, are very 'good' (Gen. 1.25). The phrase 'to tread on serpents and scorpions' targets toxic evil not reptiles. Grey squirrels translated to alien ecosystems, and goats brought to isolated islands, can do extensive, even extinctive damage. Snakes, which generally remain within their own milieu, are symbiotic members of a soil community. If Jesus the Prince of Peace brings real and not 'piecemeal peace' that peace includes predators (including the principal human predators) which follow their natures under God.

There are approximately eighty varieties of reptiles in Palestine including terrapins. While most lay eggs, a few, such as vipers, hatch within the mother. Broods of up to fifty living vipers emerge: hence the neologism (new word) viper, of William Tyndale, as a synonym for adder. Sand vipers, tolerant of extreme heat and living in the desert, prey mostly on desert rodents but occasionally, when provoked, can injure humans. More dangerous is the irascible carpet viper, also heat tolerant, which lives above ground, and like some rattlesnakes, can sidewind. Most numerous is the common Palestine viper which reaches about four feet in length and an inch in thickness. Palestine vipers appear almost everywhere except in the deserts and swamps. They frequent human settlements including Galilee. Because of their numbers and their ubiquity these common vipers inflict more damage than any other snake. Their haemotoxic (blood poisoning) venom works more slowly than that of neurotoxic (nerve poisoning) cobras which rarely migrate into central Palestine. Matthew, who refers more to snakes than do the other gospels, omits Mark's relative friendliness to reptiles in his prologue and epilogue. According to Matthew, Jesus and the Baptist describe Pharisees as a 'brood of vipers' (Mt. 12.34; 23.33), a phrase which, in Matthew's context, is not friendly to snakes. Matthew's Jesus knew that serpents, like foxes, were cunning– and for similar reasons (Mt. 10.16).

There are about twelve varieties of scorpion in Palestine, quiet, carnivorous creatures, preying mainly on insects and small mammals, and despite 'the sting in the tail', seldom fatal to humans even when trodden upon. The Lukan Jesus seemingly noticed the scorpion's unusual shape, the middle of which is sometimes egg shaped. A son seeking an egg should not receive a tripartite scorpion (Lk. 11.12).

Conclusion

We could paraphrase the Johannine community and say that if all the relationships of Jesus, to people and to other beings, were written down, the world would not contain the books written (Jn. 21.25). The creatures we have noticed within the apostolic testimony to Jesus in Palestine are *representative* of the whole earth community, everywhere and of all time, reconciled in Jesus. As enfleshed, embedded in the soil like us, Jesus contains within his humanity the whole evolving earth story. What Jesus contained, or 'assumed' in himself, has long been recognized by Christian theology as 'healed' or 'saved'. 'What is not assumed is not saved', said the Greek Fathers in the fourth century. We can rejoice that all earth creatures are included and saved in Jesus. The birds and flowers and animals around the apple trees in our gardens and in orchards recall the olive communities known to him. All these creatures, and our own domestic animals large and small, accompany us in hope on our journey into the future.

CHAPTER FIVE

Earth Spirituality with Jesus

The first Christian disciples, whom we call eyewitnesses because they lived in the time and place of Jesus, knew Jesus
successively in two ways. They knew him as a young man in the
villages and fields and by the lake during his relatively brief
public ministry in Galilee and Judea. Then, after his death and
resurrection, they knew him as risen from the dead. They also
shared their earth spirituality with Jesus in two ways. They first
prayed to the Father with Jesus when he was living among
them, a man 'like unto us'. Then, after the resurrection they
worshipped Jesus as risen, 'My Lord and my God' (Jn. 20.28),
at the centre of their lives and of the universe. We too live in and
with the risen Jesus. Neither the first disciples nor we witnessed
the resurrection itself. But we do experience Jesus in our midst
as risen Lord of the living and dead in whom all things exist.
What happens to compost in our gardens gives us 'a certain
little understanding', in a phrase of Vatican I (1869–70), of what
happens in the death and resurrection of Jesus and, later, of
ourselves. The same Jesus lives again but in a wholly new pancosmic way. As Easter people we can rejoice with the mind-
blowing musical 'Godspell', 'God is dead. Long live God'. In
our faith in the earth Jesus risen and pancosmic, we may add,

'The earth is dead. In Jesus long live the earth'. Resurrection is about life, about the earth, resurrection includes the whole earth community which, in Jesus, shares our future.

I noted in Chapter One that when I first went through the second week of the *Spiritual Exercises*, I was startled at the complete earthiness of Jesus: God really *was* and is like us in his humanity. That Indian summer week, really ten short days and sharp nights in beautiful Ohio, was my 'week of fire'. Years later when I studied Christology with James Doyle, I learned more about the fire and how to talk about the one person and two natures in Jesus. I discovered – that is, I really *realized* in my depths for the first time that, just as I contain traces of pri-mordial stardust and the earth's humus in my being, so does Jesus 'like unto us' in his complete humanity. I discovered that devotion to Jesus in his humanity, to the Sacred Heart of Jesus, is also, in an ecologically real and reverent sense, devotion to him present in the earth. To be disciples of Jesus and to share spirituality *with* him is, as St Paul wrote to the Romans, to go into the future with the other earth creatures related to us and to him in his risen humanity (Rom. 8.19–25).

When the early Jewish Christians, including eyewitnesses who had known him in the two ways just mentioned, read, on our side of the resurrection, the Jewish Scriptures, the psalms, prophets, Wisdom writings and the books attributed to Moses, they read, or heard with their hearts, these Scriptures with new insights because of what happened at Easter. They discovered clues in shadowy corners pointing to 'Galilee of the Gentiles'. In the resurrection light they beheld the Isaian portrayal of a child playing with reptiles, of Wisdom building a home on earth, and the relatively minor theme of the transformation of heaven and earth. Inspired by the living Spirit promised them by Jesus they thought and contemplated not only with their reason but in their hearts. The mind, like the night, has a thousand eyes, the day but one. But with that resurrection light, the first Christians glimpsed what eye hath not seen nor ear heard, the continuity of Jesus risen with the Jesus who lived in Palestine. I am proposing that as we live an earth spirituality with Jesus we read the Scriptures, Old Testament and New, the way the first Christians read the Jewish Scriptures – with imagination, seeking insights, enlightened by the resurrection in the power of the living Spirit.

Imaginative listening and spirituality with Jesus brings me to the title of this chapter which, of the nine chapter titles in this book, will, I suspect, appear the most curious. An earth spirituality *of* Jesus is interesting; but *with* Jesus …? In fact I mean nothing esoteric. I am simply suggesting that if imaginatively we contemplate the Scriptures *with* the present Jesus we can approach the Bible with some of the assumptions and presuppositions that he shared with the Jewish community of Palestine. Jesus grew and lived in a culture inclusive of compassion for animals, as may be seen in the famous law about not taking a mother bird and her chicks together,

> If you chance to come upon a bird's nest, in any tree or
> on the ground, with young ones or eggs and the mother
> sitting upon the young or upon the eggs, you shall not
> take the mother with the young; you shall let the mother
> go, but the young you may take to yourself; that it may
> go well with you, and that you may live long.
>
> – Deuteronomy 22.6–7

This and some other Jewish pictures can be described as conservation. And they *are* sensible conservation. But they also stir compassion as Jewish writers as different as Josephus, Philo of Alexandria, and rabbis down the centuries, testify. Anyone who has lived near animals knows that animals are relational beings who suffer, even mortally, when parted from other sensate creatures important to them. The Jews seemed to recognize this with compassion. On occasions when Jesus condoned assisting domestic animals on the Sabbath his point was compassion *for people*, but he did not exclude Jewish compassion for animals. When we engage in earth spirituality *with* Jesus we share with him the Jewish ethical tradition of compassion. Richard Bauckham writes, 'Jesus, in his recorded teaching, does not teach compassion for animals, but he places himself clearly within the Jewish ethical and legal tradition which held that God requires the people to treat their fellow creatures, the animals, with compassion and consideration.'[1] When we lack compassion for people and other fellow creatures we can ask Jesus' help in acquiring it. In a moment I shall turn to some famous texts in the Jewish Scriptures, our Old Testament, which were also familiar to Jesus, which he used in his teaching, and about which we can pray with him.

Imaginative dialogue

But first another word about biblical science. Since the seventeenth-century scientific awakening biblical scholars, or exegetes, have explored the Bible exhaustively, deploying historical, linguistic, literary, textual and archaeological tools. Adapting some of the methods of modern physical and social sciences they have helped us read the Bible. But only recently have they begun to recognize that *reading*, even sacred reading, is also a *dialogue* to which living readers contribute. Even physical scientists and professional historians now recognize that the most clinically controlled laboratory investigation is time and context – and scientist – conditioned. The most clinical scientists are never wholly detached, nor disembedded, to use a current term. Neither scientists nor exegetes, nor we who contemplate our heritage, are immune from prejudice. We are culturally embedded in our planet, influenced by received wisdoms of our time and place, and surfeited with information by media which also limit what is communicated. Exegetes are limited by the specific questions they are moved to ask for a limited moment in history which, during the high tide of biblical scholarship, has been an excessively anthropocentric time. In a word, biblical scholars no less than the rest of us are in dialogue with the Bible; their attitudes, interests and questions contributing to the texts they survey. Where we may differ from some exegetes is that we know and accept that we are prejudiced. Prejudices can be good. One of our 'prejudices' is that Jesus is the centre of earth spirituality. To Jesus we look for an earth spirituality which we can share with him and with each other. Jesus is the Alpha and Omega of God's Word to us today. Virginia University's Robert Louis Wilken notes,

> Through history, Christ transforms history, and after his coming a strictly historical interpretation of the Old Testament is anachronistic. For the Scriptures can no longer be interpreted as one interprets other documents from the past, setting things in historical context, deciding what came earlier and what later, relating things to what went before or followed afterward. Now interpretation must begin at the centre which is also the beginning and the end, with Christ who is the Alpha and the Omega.[2]

[75]

Jesus not a conservationist

But here a word of caution. Jesus is the centre of our earth spirituality through whom we approach God in the midst of the earth community. But in his life on earth Jesus was not a conservationist, ecologist, nor environmentalist in our contemporary sense. To imagine Jesus immune from cultural boundaries would be anachronistic, it would not be *perceptive* imagination at all, it would project into the apostolic testimonies a green face that was never really there. The Jesus whom we imaginatively contemplate, and with whom we live an earth spirituality, lived in iron age Palestine when technologies were relatively basic and sustainable, animals numerous and on the land, their manure appreciated and used, and human numbers and impact within the carrying capacities of local ecosystems. Living briefly in this Roman world Jesus, while sensitive to the natural world and its ways, was not an environmentalist in our modern sense. Nor did he foresee silent springs ahead.

His sensitivity to nature, so vivid in his parables, derived from living close to the natural world and from familiarity with the Jewish Scriptures and their metaphors of cosmic order, drawn from predictably changing seasons, reliable skies and winds, seas which did not transgress the limits of the strand, birds which migrated seasonally in autumn and on the spring thermals. People alone, God's responsible delegates on earth, transgress those limits as recklessly as a horse plunging into battle, bringing nemesis and God's judgement, upon the human malefactor and his fellow earthlings. A prophetic text to which Jesus may have listened at home, in the synagogue or at school is the pictorial description by Jeremiah of birds migrating seasonally in contrast to the arrogant rebellion of human creatures,

> Even the stork in the heavens
> knows her times;
> and the turtledove, swallow, and crane
> keep the time of their coming;
> but my people know not
> the ordinance of the Lord.
>
> – Jeremiah 8.7

Although Jesus lived within a Jewish culture of compassion for people and all other beings he does not, as Bauckham observes, explicitly *teach* compassion for animals and plants but, in his parables, presupposes it. To teach that compassion is *a fortiori* (even more) due to people still *implies* compassion for *animals*! The breadth of his Father's compassion is expressed beautifully by the psalmist,

> The Lord is good to all,
> and his compassion is over all that
> he has made.
>
> – Psalm 145.9

When Jesus defends healing on the Sabbath, he compares his action with Jewish compassion for domestic animals. 'Does not each of you on the Sabbath untie his ox or his ass from the manger, and lead it away to water it? And ought not this woman, a daughter of Abraham whom Satan bound for eighteen years, be loosed from this bond on the Sabbath day?' (Lk. 13.15–16). What we today call 'the economy' was not the only reason a Jewish countryman cared for his domestic animals. So while we affirm that Jesus was neither a conservationist nor an ecologist in our modern sense, we nevertheless may say that in his recognition of his own unique importance for God's

[77]

kingdom and in his inclusive compassion, Jesus was the first Christian ecologist! When we contemplate the earth Jesus in his life in Palestine we do not discover a green face at the bottom of a dark well, but we do behold a Jesus with whom we can share our earth spirituality.

The Jesus with whom we pray in Palestine was circumscribed by the cultural limits of rural and village life. In modern eco-theological speak, we may say that Jesus was, as we try to be, anthropocentric but not anthroposolic: human creatures are supremely important but other creatures, while they are also for human use, have their own value and glorify God in their own ways. Fig and fruit trees deserve care, but if they don't produce they may be felled and burned. Weeds invading cultivated fields may be uprooted, bundled, and used for fuel. Olives, vines and the whole variety of seeds are good in themselves and for human use. Jesus speaks often and appreciatively of sheep but accepts, and apparently participates in, ritual sacrifice. He tolerates Jewish ritual exclusiveness of swine and dogs. Nor is he described as objecting to fishermen discarding unsuitable fish. Like ourselves he is portrayed as reasonably wary of reptiles, scorpions and wolves. What emerges from the gospels is a villager within the Jewish tradition of holistic compassion and sustainable organic husbandry with people and animals on the land, working with and not against the ways of nature.

There are, it must be admitted, some difficult texts in the Scriptures, including encouragement of ethnic cleansing such as 1 Samuel 15.2–3. There are difficult stories even in the gospels such as the Gadarene swine and the unfortunate fig tree. We accept these stories as included within the canon. We do not attempt to ignore, suppress or 'ditch' them. When a text seems to contravene the general tone of respect for God's creatures, when it endorses exploitation not only of animals and plants but even (in the Old Testament) of peoples, I suggest that awkward texts be read not in isolation but within the whole canon of the Bible. The Church includes seemingly discordant texts within the canon. In other words, there is a *canonical* sense to a text because the text is received and contemplated within the whole canon. God's compassion for all that he has made is repeated throughout the Bible, 'He gives to the beasts their food, and to the young ravens which cry' (Ps. 147.9). But in pictures of the Gadarene swine and the fig tree, for example, God in Jesus seems almost indifferent to his creatures. We have to weigh the difficult, even discordant, texts and then come to a decision as to what God is teaching us in the whole canonical Bible. Raymond Brown writes, 'Whether consciously or unconsciously, the Church has placed side by side in the same canon works that do not share the same outlook. The response to the canon is not to suppress or undervalue the sharp view of an individual biblical author, but to make up one's mind in face of diverse views existing side by side.[3]

Jesus, Genesis and Lynn White, Jr.

Not only is Jesus within the Jewish ethical tradition of compassion, he is also familiar with some of the ecological texts in the Jewish Scriptures which most interest us today. When we reflect upon the sense and connotations of these texts we can do so in communion with Jesus. When debating with other Jews about marriage and divorce, Jesus referred to the closing verses of the prose poem which prefaces Genesis. Jesus referred especially to the words that God had created mankind male and female, combining these with the similar, more primitive creation text in Genesis 2. 'From the beginning of creation, "God

[79]

made them male and female". For this reason a man shall leave his father and mother and be joined to his wife, and the two shall become one flesh so they are no longer two but one flesh. What therefore God has joined together, let not man put asunder' (Mk. 10.6–9; Mt. 19.3–6).

Earth spirituality includes responding to false interpretations of our heritage, but with repentance. In a famous, oft-quoted article, the medieval historian Lynn White, Jr., indicted Christianity for the ecological crisis. White and his followers refer to the Genesis creation accounts as condoning exploitation of a devalued, 'human resource', natural world,

> We shall continue to have a worsening ecological crisis until we reject the Christian axiom that nature has no reason for existence but to serve man…. Both our present science and technology are so tinctured with orthodox Christian arrogance towards nature that no solution for our ecological crisis can be expected from them alone.[4]

Others have responded to White.[5] I would add that critics who indict Christians for earth abuse are both right and wrong. They are right that Christian and post-Christian societies, with a substantial Christian presence, have done perhaps terminal damage to the earth, and even now are apathetic about earth healing. We cannot deny the truth of J. B. Priestley's observation that there is something very wrong with a people who destroy a coast the way the English have disfigured the south coast from Portsmouth to Dover. Similar indictments are true of other societies with other coasts. Of American society Robert Frost said, 'it doesn't take long to destroy a continent'. Yet despite undeniable exploitation of fellow creatures in Christian and post-Christian societies, Lynn White, Jr., and others who indict Christianity *itself* as premier eco-villain, are wrong. Our fault lies not in our heritage but in our infidelity to our well-springs, including the Genesis text, cited by White and others, which we pray with Jesus. The 'increase and multiply and sub-due' text, *within its context*, portrays people not as earth tramplers but as God's image with responsibilities under God to let be. Exploitation of God's earth by his image is absolutely forbidden. The text cited by White and his fellow critics, far from endorsing earth abuse and runaway procreation, puts humanity in our place under God with responsibilities for other creatures. The climax of the prose poem is not the human arrival but the Sabbath rest and worship. The fecundity blessing to increase and multiply and fill the earth, writes the German Catholic exegete Norbert Lohfink, 'is not to be regarded as a blessing upon all men for all time. It is aimed at the establishment of the people, and so it flows directly into the phrase "and fill the earth".'[6]

When we reflect prayerfully upon Genesis with Jesus we participate in a reflection in which he engaged in his life on earth. What emerges within Genesis and the whole canonical Bible is an appreciation of men and women as responsible sovereign creatures who flourish best together with responsibilities to God *and* to one another. For Jesus adds, 'What therefore God has joined together, let not man put asunder' (Mt. 19.6). These responsibilities extend to the whole peopled kingdom. An attractive picture of responsibilities for other people and for the whole earth community is that of the idealized Maccabean ruler Simon who ruled near the time of Jesus. Lynn White, Jr., no less than we, should listen to the whole canon!

They tilled their land in peace;
the ground gave its increase,
and the trees of the plains their fruit.
Old men sat in the streets;
they talked together of good things,
and the youths put on splendid military attire.
He supplied the towns with food,
and furnished them with the means of defence,
until his renown spread to the ends of the earth.
He established peace in the land,
and Israel rejoiced with great joy.
All the people sat under their own vines and fig trees,
and there was none to make them afraid …
He made the sanctuary glorious,
and added to the vessels of the sanctuary.

– 1 Maccabees 14.8–15

Psalm 8

An interesting hymn, one which exalts humanity while celebrating God the Supreme Sovereign enjoying his creation, is Psalm 8. We contemplate this beautiful poem with Jesus knowing that, according to Matthew, Jesus explicitly quoted it when he entered Jerusalem for the last time. Jesus rode into the city on a donkey, a provocative entrance that would to some Jews connote an awaited future king,

Lo, your king comes to you;
 triumphant and victorious is he,
humble and riding on an ass,
 on a colt the foal of an ass.

– Zechariah 9.9

[82]

When, after the controversial episode in the temple, children hailed him as Son of David, to the annoyance of the establishment, Jesus quoted Psalm 8, 'Out of the mouth of babes and sucklings thou hast brought perfect praise' (Mt. 21.16; Ps. 8.2). This short, beautiful, cosmic hymn, with its exalted anthropology, gives us another and distinctively royal picture of humans within God's biodiverse kingdom. In other parts of the ancient world, in the Nile valley and in parts of Mesopotamia, the planets, trees, sea creatures and large animals were regarded as fertility symbols or even divine. Not so in Psalm 8. When with Jesus we contemplate the known cosmos with wonder we recognize that humans, under God, rule earth creatures as in a garden which is not our own possession. Plants and other animals, even the most sublime, are subject to human dominion. Humans in turn are responsible to God. Our rule is subservient, with justice and peace. The psalm begins and ends with an inclusive refrain rejoicing in God the sovereign creator and Lord of the earth, 'O Lord, our Lord, how majestic is thy name in all the earth!' (Ps. 8.1, 9). The anonymous writer of the letter to the Hebrews prays this psalm with us, recognizing, long before our feast of Christ the King, that Jesus risen is alone completely sovereign over all things. 'We see Jesus, who for a little while was made lower than the angels, crowned with glory and honour because of the suffering of death, so that by the grace of God he might taste death for every one' (Heb. 2.9).

The rainbow covenant
Jesus refers to the flood story in a warning about the suddenness of judgement (Mt. 24.36–44; Lk. 17.26–33). The flood literature includes pictures of human relationships with animals. In the earlier Genesis creation stories we have a vegetarian

ideal, 'I have given you every plant yielding seed which is upon the face of all the earth, and every tree with seed in its fruit; you shall have them for food' (Gen. 1.29). The flood sequence – or compromise – is more realistic, truer to life as we know it. After the waters recede, Noah offers God a sacrifice of clean birds and animals which pleases God, who then stabilizes the cosmos. 'While the earth remains, seedtime and harvest, cold and heat, summer and winter, day and night, shall not cease' (Gen. 8.22). God permits people – and other sensate beings – to eat meat but not the blood which symbolizes life which belongs to God. This uneasy compromise is pictured in the rainbow covenant. God enters a covenant with humans *and the (other) animals* promising that he will not destroy the earth community again with raging waters. 'Behold, I establish my covenant with you and your descendants after you, and with every living creature that is with you, the birds, the cattle, and every beast of the earth with you, as many as came out of the ark' (Gen. 9.9–10). So closely bound are we to our fellow animal creatures that we are in a covenant with God, with animals as covenant partners. To be covenant partners is to have relationships with the animals and implicitly with other living creatures. The rainbow in the sky is a reminder of our bond with other creatures. We are all, at least metaphorically, rainbow warriors on their behalf.

The author of Hebrews relates the 'everlasting' rainbow covenant to Jesus and to blood sacrifice. 'May the God of peace who brought again from the dead our Lord Jesus, the great shepherd of the sheep, by the blood of the eternal covenant, equip you with everything good' (Heb. 13.20–21). From the flood story through Hebrews and later, the Roman and Gallican liturgies, 'the everlasting covenant' has entered our western eucharistic liturgies. When we offer 'the blood of the new and everlasting covenant' we are in continuity with the rainbow covenant and Jesus' references to Noah in the context of sudden judgement. We may reflect with Jesus on our relationships with animals in an 'everlasting covenant'. There is an echo of that relationship at every Eucharist which, at the consecration, recalls the new and 'everlasting' covenant. Animals, especially those we have known in our brief days on earth share our future. My pekes have a point in their unshakeable assumption that we are partners and companions forever. The everlasting covenant includes them.

Melchizedek

The Genesis stories, Psalm 8, and the flood draw much of their imagery, their earth spirituality and ecological wisdom, from other ancient religions. The Jewish religion of Jesus was one minority religion among many. The mysterious Melchizedek, king of Salem, who appears briefly in Genesis and then disappears into the mists, lives on in our tradition, our Eucharists, our ordination rites. Melchizedek and Abraham represent the other religions which share our earth, and our faith in God the creator. Jesus quotes Psalm 110 which includes Melchizedek the mysterious priest king who blesses Abraham with bread and wine (Mk. 12.35-7). We associate our priesthood with him when we celebrate ordinations with reference to 'the order of Melchizedek'. We know very little about him, a mysterious sacral sovereign who blesses Abraham with bread and wine in the valley of the kings and vanishes into the mists. Yet we feel an affinity with this shadowy stranger. We are people of the bread and wine through which we offer the whole earth community, in Christ Jesus, to God. Melchizedek, like Jesus and ourselves, is a person of the bread and wine.

[85]

Today we are looking for ways to co-operate and share earth spirituality with other religions while remaining faithful to our own. Melchizedek and Abraham, who with bread and wine shared earth spiritualities, are representative of these other religions. Melchizedek, in the only prayer attributed to him, praises God, creator of heaven and earth, 'Blessed be Abraham by God Most High, maker of heaven and earth.' Abraham responded, 'I have sworn to the Lord God Most High, maker of heaven and earth' (Gen. 14.18–23). No one religion, no one earth spirituality, can heal and restore God's earth today. But all the religions, of which Abraham and Melchizedek are representatives, and humanism too, can make a difference. In the words of Pope John Paul II, 'The most pressing issues facing humanity – ecology, peace, the co-existence of different races and cultures, for example, – may possibly be solved if there is collaboration between Christians and followers of other religions and all who while not sharing religious faith seek human renewal.'

Conclusion

Everywhere people say they are looking for an earth spirituality, a spirituality in and with the earth community in which God is immanent and loving and inviting earth healing. We have treasures in our heritage which, when we have 'made it our own', we can share with all people. Jesus risen is our future and the future of the whole earth community with which we are related and bound in an everlasting covenant. In his life *before* the resurrection, Jesus contemplated some important ecological texts which now instruct us. With imagination, seeking discoveries, and listening with the ears of the heart, we contemplate those same texts in *his presence today*. We can and do share our earth spirituality with Jesus.

[86]

CHAPTER SIX

The Family and the Earth

Every year the brightness of the daffodils and, in autumn, the colourful ripening of the plums reminds me that we living beings are an earth community. In all seasons, when working in my front garden, I notice how people, especially children, enjoy exchanging greetings with my peke companions. Most of us like animals, but children, especially before adolescence, almost inhabit an ark. They relate naturally to furry and feathery and watery creatures. To children, says Mary Midgely, 'animals are an innate taste'. Children learn more about wildlife and domestic animals in their own fruit and vegetable gardens, and in parks and fields, than from tarmac to tarmac holidays. If parents and teachers and others nourish children's innate taste for other life they will be forever sensitive to the earth as community. If we fail to teach and encourage them, their adulthood may centre not on community, but on marketing, competition, plastic, and machines.

In reality, the primary community is neither the family, the Church, nor society, but the whole soil or earth community, whatever flies in the sky, moves in the waters and dwells on the land, and their many habitats. The earth is the primary community with which we have to reintegrate and to whose economy we must adjust. In Herbert Girardet's words, 'instead of adjusting nature to fit in with our behaviour patterns we have to adjust our economic practices to be compatible with the natural world.' We need to recover our childhood taste for animals, to wonder at the yellow daffodils and purple plums. We need to remind ourselves that other beings too are other, with needs of their own which make demands on us. Our loss of a sense of community with them, and the widespread disintegration of the family community, are not unrelated.

During an interdisciplinary seminar on the family a few years ago I noticed how narrow, almost earth exclusive, can be specialities related to the family. I realized how we need to reconstruct, in an earth-inclusive way, not only theology but the social sciences, child psychology, educational science, and Christian ethics. We who think we are modern or even postmodern can learn from wise women in local Mothers' Unions and Women's Institutes who make the connections between the family and the earth almost as innately as children relate to my peke and pond. The primary, fundamental, or all inclusive, 'justice and peace' is due to the whole earth within which is human 'justice and peace', the primary 'mission and ministry' is to respond to the disintegration of local and global ecosystems upon which all families and all people depend. The primary 'culture of death' is the accelerating death of wetlands, fields and habitats, and therefore of local people, here at home, and the tourism, logging and mining of soil fertility abroad in which we are implicated. The primary 'liturgy and justice' includes the whole earth community.

Active contemplation

Exploring our heritage imaginatively leads to discoveries which will not be stranded like a boat on shingle after the tide goes out. Imaginative exploration makes connections. We find clues in our heritage about our relationships and responsibilities. Our discoveries will become part of a holistic Christian ethos helping family life to recuperate within a healthy earth. We can explore, among other dimensions of our heritage, the Bible. Each generation with its own distinctive needs will find different treasures in the Bible which respond to those needs. Manlio Simonetti says,

> The history of doctrine is the history of exegesis, in that the whole development of catholic doctrine is based on the interpretation of a certain number of passages in Scripture in the light of particular needs; but the same could be said of any other aspect of the Church's life: organization, discipline, worship.[1]

Our own 'particular needs' at a time of disturbed family life require more than the urban, limited, and ecologically inadequate methods of most recent biblical scholarship. Richard Bauckham of St Andrews University observes,

> It is becoming painfully obvious that much modern interpretation of the New Testament has been consciously and unconsciously influenced by the prevalent ideology of the modern West which for two centuries or so has understood human history as emancipation from nature.[2]

In rejecting the current ideology that people are emancipated somehow from the rest of nature, and free to 'develop' nature evermore at home and overseas, I am not suggesting that we read family earth spirituality *into* the Bible, but that we behold imaginatively what is there. Imagination puts flesh and visage into the bare bones of what we discover. Imagination, says Noel Dermot O'Donaghue, 'perceives what is really there, though it comes, like all perceptions, not only as a pure datum something given, but in a fruitful marriage of what is in the mind and what is outside it.'[3] There are hints of family in the Bible which point like trajectories to the inclusion of the elderly, children, single people and neighbours, and domestic animals and pets, within the family community. Contemplating family relationships pictured in the Bible we discover the earth-inclusiveness of good kings and good families. We notice that human justice and rightness includes good relationships with all earth creatures. When we sin relationships are disrupted. We suffer along with our fellow creatures. When we strive to do right they too flourish enjoying sun and sweet rain,

> Be glad, O sons of Zion,
> and rejoice in the Lord, your God;
> for he has given the early rain for your vindication,
> he has poured down for you abundant rain,
> the early and the latter rain, as before.
>
> – Joel 2.23

The creation stories and family

There are hints and pointers to family community from the first pages of the Bible. The blessing to procreate which our species has accepted with some enthusiasm, first given to Adam and Eve, already a primordial family, in the garden, is repeated after the flood to Noah's patriarchal family and to pairs of sensate beings who shared the ark (Gen. 8.17). When relatively few people become numerous enough to occupy and till a land and become a people, when, from Dan to Beer-Sheba, every man sits at peace under his own fruit, the blessing to multiply is

6 · THE FAMILY AND THE EARTH

accomplished. There is no encouragement for *excessive* procreation and socially and environmentally ruinous migrations in the Bible (Ex. 1.7 f).

As Simonetti says, succeeding generations will find 'certain passages' of Scripture – and I would add certain dimensions of the whole living tradition – relevant for the 'particular needs' of their own time. For *our* time the flood sequence is such a passage. We now see references to 'the ark' almost everywhere. It speaks to people today, even those on the edge and beyond our tradition. According to the ancient story a few pairs of people occupied the ark with pairs, or more, of animals and birds. When the waters receded and Noah with his patriarchal family disembarked these few people did not reinhabit a dualistic earth with people divided from fellow creatures, rather 'every beast, every creeping thing, and every bird, everything that moves upon the earth, went forth by families out of the ark' (Gen. 8.19). As at hominization, the evolution of conscious human creatures, in this post-diluvial (after the flood) new beginning, people are inherently and forever related to other beings upon whom we depend and who depend upon us. The rediscovery of the rainbow by our generation is especially precious, reminding people that we *and the animals* are related to each other and to God in 'an earth community' (Gen. 9.12–17). We not only have relationships with animals as fellow subjects, but also with the flora upon which we and the animals depend and which we cultivate, sometimes with their help and manure. In the colourful rainbow covenant 'our common future' includes the whole biodiverse and extended earth community. As the waters recede, Noah, the first gardener, plants a vineyard where he lives with his dependants among the fruits of the vines and the trees. Family relationships within the earth, especially with the olive community, are renewed as people, and the animals, again procreate and reinhabit God's earth.

A righteous person in the culture from which Jesus came shared harvests with the wider earth community including widows, orphans, sojourners, and wild and domestic animals (Ex. 23.9–12). One of the anguished Job's visitors, Eliphaz the Temanite, remarked that a righteous man lives at peace with animals and even with stones, a reference to working with the soil in rocky terrain where seed easily 'falls upon stony ground',

> At destruction and famine you shall laugh,
>   and shall not fear the beasts of the earth.
> For you shall be in league with the
>   stones of the field,
> and the beasts of the field shall be
>   at peace with you.
>
> – Job 5.22–3

Rural Jews realized – as do modern urbanites with grey squirrels around – that wild animals compete with humans for harvests, water, habitats and space, and that some threaten domestic animals. They were not conscious that people – even then – were a threat to the very survival of whole species of wild animals, as our generation now realizes. The Jews did anticipate future harmony with animals. Some expected a Davidic king who would secure symbiosis among people, their domestic animals and wild creatures. A poem familiar to us, composed during exile, is our best known and most vivid portrayal of the awaited peaceable kingdom. In the poem youngsters consort with predators: even serpents live at peace with children. The very hearing of the poem read aloud, as in Advent liturgies, warms our hearts with hope. There may be a hint of dominion in the child's gentle leadership of the animals, but it is a dominion *with* the wild animals, co-operative letting be, not domination. The imagery of vegetarianism – lions eat straw, serpents dust – reminds us of the first verses of Genesis, stirring in us a hope for a future in which predation and war cease. Neither the poem nor its summary in Isaiah 65.25 explicitly includes the human family – yet the centrality of the child surely implies parenting and the human family,

> The wolf shall dwell with the lamb,
>> and the leopard shall lie down with the kid,
> and the calf and the lion and the fatling together,
>> and a little child shall lead them.
> The cow and the bear shall feed;
>> their young shall lie down together;
>> and the lion shall eat straw like the ox.
> The sucking child shall play over the
>> hole of the asp,
>> and the weaned child shall put his
>> hand on the adder's den.
> They shall not hurt or destroy
>> in all my holy mountain;
> for the earth shall be full of the knowledge of the Lord
> as the waters cover the sea.
>
> – Isaiah 11.6–9

Into the New Testament

There are in the New Testament, in Christian art and early testimonies, numerous references relating the young Jesus to Nazareth and family life in the hill country. Mark, who has no infancy stories, says simply that Jesus 'came from Nazareth' to the Baptist at the Jordan (Mk. 1.9). Matthew says that after the sojourn in Egypt the holy family 'went and dwelt in a city called

Nazareth, that what was spoken by the prophets might be fulfilled, "He shall be called a Nazarene"' (Mt. 2.23; Isa. 11.1). Luke adds the familiar story of the young boy lost in the temple who returned with his parents to Nazareth 'their own city' where he was subject to them (Lk. 2.39, 41–51). In later life, after he had left home, Jesus again returned to Nazareth 'where he had been raised' (Lk. 4.16–20). John who, like Mark, has no infancy narrative, connects Jesus with both Bethlehem *and* Nazareth. 'Is the Christ to come from Galilee? Has not the scripture said that the Christ is descended from David, and comes from Bethlehem, the village where David was?' (Jn. 7.41–2). John refers again to Nazareth in the only words we know were written about Jesus in his lifetime, the trilingual words on the cross: 'Jesus of Nazareth King of the Jews' (Jn. 19.19). This written insult, by an adamant Gentile named Pilate – what he had written he had written – has royal as well as family connotations. At least one of Jesus' family was with him when he died. Jesus, says John, entrusted his mother to the disciple he loved. John adds 'in the place where he was crucified there was a garden', a hint of the original garden where the first man and woman, whom God had joined together, lived peacefully with other creatures (Jn. 19.26–7, 41).

Reconciliation in Jesus of Nazareth, risen and glorified, includes all families and all creatures, the entire earth community, past, present and future. The resurrection is the initial transformation of the cosmos, of our families and of ourselves, the beginning of the peaceable kingdom.

Worship and sacraments

Families, within which I include here all those persons to whom a man and woman are related, what is sometimes called the extended family, pray together at certain times especially on feasts, Sabbaths and in key moments in life for which we have sacraments or rites of passage. Praying together *as families* certainly strengthens family life and friendship. By reflecting together on the significance of the Sabbath in the Jewish Scriptures, and in testimonies to Jesus, we discover insights for our worship today in our time of family and earth need. The recognition of Sunday as special, as a time of prayer and community – the Lord's day (Ex. 20.10) – has, by 'keeping Sunday special' in consumer societies, become a counter-cultural sign, even a living gospel: the Sabbath is not for work and shopping, not for 'marketing', but work and 'the market' for the Sabbath. Sunday rest and worship remind us that families are not for work, but work for the good of families. Sabbath people, with their wild and domestic animals, owe allegiance neither to advertizing nor to the market. Work, including church work, misunderstood, can take people away from the Eucharist, it can separate parents from children, it can destroy the environment which supports life. The Sabbath, all worship, and all family prayer illuminate as with a beacon the real purpose of human work. At a Youth Conference in Rimini, Pope John Paul II said perceptively, 'The ecological catastrophe confronting humanity is profoundly ethical in the forgetfulness of the true nature of human work, especially of its subjective dimension, its value for the family and society.'[4]

The sacramental rites

Jesus' baptism symbolically sanctified the Jordan and all the waters of the world. All water sacramentally is the Jordan. The eastern churches ritually celebrate the sacramentality of water. Jacob of Serugh, an early Syrian ascetic, wrote beautifully, 'seas, deeps, rivers, springs and pools all thronged together to receive the blessing from your footsteps.'[5] The sacredness of water prompts us to respect, and where necessary heal, seas, beaches and all local aquifers with their teeming life, even rainwater is precious. Families, including friends and relatives who sponsor the newly baptized, can draw water from local aquifers and return baptismal water to the soil perhaps near a baptismal tree. Water and trees symbolize life, water is life, whole cultures celebrate the tree of life. God's Wisdom, with whom the early Christians identified Jesus, was described as 'a tree of life to those who lay hold of her; those who hold fast to her are called happy' (Prov. 3.18). Baptismal trees, especially indigenous or fruit trees, symbolize our baptism into new life in the risen Christ, we are baptized *into* and not away from the earth.

Confirmation, whether before or after first communion, is an important initiation rite, especially today when to be a Christian we need strength and openness to the living Spirit. We live as Christians in a time when people try to live without God, and when even among Christians there is much 'partial disaffiliation' or sitting loose to church customs. Living as Christians in a time of individualism requires courage, strength, the experience of God's Spirit. Many people, not all of them Christians, sacrifice comfort, even their lives, for the earth community, as for example, in the rain forests, in wildlife reservations and in peaceful protests about bull and bird abuse, animal exports, road and runway construction, militarism, and careless genetic engineering. As baptized and confirmed in Christ, we need to be prepared to sacrifice, to consume sustainably and locally, to share transport, to holiday sustainably in our own bioregions (as, for example, in northern Europe for one living in the UK) and not engage in environmentally ruinous tourism, even if described as pilgrimage, and to give time and effort to restore habitats in our own neighbourhoods. Confirmation trees *in* our neighbourhoods are a symbol of healing and strength in Christ.

At the Eucharist we are privileged to worship as communities, offering the reconciled cosmos in Christ to God. In a Catholic eucharistic prayer we say, 'all creation rightly gives you praise, all life, all holiness comes from you'. The whole earth community is included in bread and wine as it is in our bodies. The Eucharist makes us peacemakers, for militarism destroys the fields where grain and grapes grow and the children who are always wars' losers, whether living today or tomorrow. We can beat offensive weapons into sustainable hospitals, schools, housing, orchards, wheatfields and habitats. As families we offer 'bread which earth has given and human hands have made' and wine 'fruit of the vine and work of human hands'. We should use local organic bread and wine at our Eucharists. The Lutheran liturgical theologian Gordon Lathrop writes of the local Eucharist,

> Bread unites the fruitful goodness of the earth with the ancient history of human cultivation. Bread represents the earth and the rain, growing grains, sowing and reaping, milling and baking, together with the mystery of yeast.... The translucent liquid also holds together the fruitful earth, the sun and the rain, the ancient history of human cultivation, and the mystery of yeast and fermentation. It also is a food that has been made in endless local varieties, bearing the mark of local cultures. It too is meant for a group – the cup for sharing, the bottle too much for one – and seems to be misused when drunk alone. Here, poured out for a human circle, there flows the goodness of the earth pressed out, the sun made liquid.[6]

[97]

Locally grown organic bread and wine unite the eucharistic community with local family farmers, with local soil fertility, wildlife and habitats. Local produce eliminates earth-damaging long-distance food transport (food miles). Local organic bread and wine were used by Jesus and the first Christians.

Penance, unction and our penitential prayers should include personal and structural ecological sin with which we, as a counter-cultural people, cannot co-operate: questionable arms and tobacco trade, unnecessary construction, socially and environmentally damaging tourism, and the manipulative media, whether religious or secular, none of which have we adequately challenged. When we 'call to mind our sins', therefore, let us include our own participation in structural ecological sin. The words of Alan Gear, chief executive of HDRA (the UK national centre for organic growing) deserve prayerful, even repentant consideration,

> It is a scandal that organic-phosphate insecticides should ever have had any place whatsoever in food production. How anyone could have imagined that a group of compounds originally manufactured as chemical weapons that attacked the nervous system, could be sprayed on to crops and animals and not have an adverse effect on human health, is beyond my comprehension. Yet, despite an alarming body of evidence, there are still no official moves to ban them.[7]

The patenting of animals and plants and even human genes, engineering herbicide tolerant crops, modifying seeds so that growers, including small holders, cannot save seed for the following year – these and other manipulations of life and food are morally questionable. Through 'perverse subsidies' of industrial farming we have let families be forced off small farms and into towns. Perverse subsidies which encourage family and earth damaging practices and which maximize construction and fossil fuel use by cars and planes, at the expense of sustainable transport, are the concern of people who are God's representatives on earth. Harmful things are done to farmers and to our soil so that in the short term we may purchase apparently cheap food on large store shelves for ourselves and our families. In the *short* term! Are we not structurally implicated when damage is done to small farmers here and overseas, to our soil and seeds, our countryside, wildlife and habitats, and to our food? Companies which manipulate seeds and animals and plants experiment with the death of birth. They, and no longer God, say 'let there be life'. Can we with impunity enjoy apparently cheap food from such companies? Should we encourage wasteful packaging and unnecessarily imported food at out of town multiple retailers? Ecological sins can be family sins which damage the elderly, children, and the future of families. Infrastructure projects such as ever more bypasses which attract ever more cars destroying ever more fields, large runways, dams, marinas, holiday villages may involve us in structural sin. What would happen, we could almost say what will happen, when Chinese and Indian people travel like Americans, Japanese and affluent European families? The way we live as families may demand family repentance, a change of family lifestyle which will bring its own happiness. Some working for overseas development funds may ask themselves if their air travel is always really necessary. Is 'development' which excludes the welfare of the whole earth really justice? Social justice without ecological justice is injustice which ultimately injures people. Ecological injustice requires restitution, perhaps through financial and personal support of local conservationists and their projects. Commemorative trees and glades, fruit trees and orchards, voluntary service in local wildlife groups, support of local growers, energy-efficient homes, churches and schools effectively symbolize our healing of God's earth.

Death is not escape of the soul from the earth. Rather in death we become pancosmic, more united to the whole earth, including our own bodies, than in this life. Our funeral and burial rites should symbolize death as life in and with the universe. Woodland cemeteries, green burials, and contributions to inclusive charities in lieu of flowers at funerals, symbolize the pancosmic and eternal life which begins at death. A prayer of Benedictine Sister Ancilla Dent, naturalist of Minster Abbey, Kent, is useful at funerals, in penitential services, public and private, and at the Eucharist and all rites of passage,

> O God enlarge within us
> > a sense of fellowship with all living things
> > to whom you gave the earth in common with us.
> May we live gently with our fellow creatures
> > and through the work of our hands
> > may the voice of the earth go up to you
> > not in sorrow but in a song of praise.

> *– adapted from* ST BASIL

The Church's ministry, 'holy orders', is often the visible profile of the Church to people outside and to many within. The *ecological* witness of ministers, deacons, priests and bishops, in lifestyle and in transport, in ordination liturgies and in homilies, in daily ministries large and small, represents all of us. The importance of earth-inclusive liturgies, intercessions at the Eucharist, homilies and catechesis by commissioned ministers of Christ in the Church, cannot be exaggerated. Through an ordained ministry, which in its visible leadership includes the cosmic dimension of Christ and salvation, the holistic depths of the living tradition flow visibly into 'the preaching and life of the believing and praying Church' (Constitution on Divine Revelation, 8). Permanent deacons – and similarly commissioned ministers – are, at least potentially, Christian ecological leaders. The deacon's ministry historically has been liturgy, word and charity, a comprehensive ministry especially related to the Eucharist.[8] Deacons can – and I have suggested often that they should – represent the commissioned ministry and all of us, God's priestly people, in ministry to local environmentalists, as in living churchyard and commemorative tree ministries. Deacons can assist us to integrate worship, beginning with intercessions and homilies, with local wildlife and gardening groups, with conservationists, and with the United Nations Association which deserve the support of Christians and inclusion in our earth spirituality.

Marriage sanctifies the union of man and woman to which Jesus referred when he said a man leaves his parents and adheres to his wife (Mk. 10.7; Mt. 19.5). When we who are married pray together, especially when we include neighbours and others in our extended families, we are the cosmos at prayer, we pray in the name of the whole earth community including our plants and animals. Interestingly the third-century Roman deacon, Hippolytus, knew married Christians in that city who prayed together when one day ended and another began,

> The elders who transmitted the tradition taught that at this hour the whole creation rests for a moment to praise the Lord: stars, trees, waters stop for a moment,

and the whole host of ministering angels, to praise God
together with the souls of the just.

– Apostolic Tradition 41

With the expanding need to *nurture* elderly people and children, dedicated single people, whether in religious life or in the
midst, are needed as rarely before. Single people can minister in
solidarity with married persons. Married persons with few or
no biological children who, together with single persons, nurture elderly people and children, including handicapped and
fostered children, and all creation great and small, are within an
alternative marriage community which we may call cosmic marriage. That is, childless married couples, with single people,
and with married people with children, may care for the whole
earth community and the future. We need inclusive marriage
rituals and ceremonies for renewal of marriage commitment
symbolizing the *extended* family so needed in this our time.

Conclusion
Women and men today are looking for a marriage spirituality
for an alternative community, in continuity with but different
from, the nuclear family of earlier this century. An earth spirituality should include the extended family – and that extension
includes more than blood relations and more even than people.
My wife Barbara and I, and, of course, our peke, have tried to
widen our 'family circle' and family spirituality. What we have
done and are doing is in many ways breaking new ground,
sometimes literally! Others can, and doubtless will, improve on
our lived alternatives. To these I shall return.

CHAPTER SEVEN

Jesus and the Post-Martians

It may seem strange to include a chapter on extraterrestrials in an earth spirituality book! In fact when I told a feminist friend I planned to include one, she said she was more concerned that we are raising children in 'a damaged land' here on earth, in our time. She quoted Ortega y Gasset's words, 'Tell me the landscape in which you live and I will tell you who you are'. Yet the pluralist hypothesis (that there may *be* other inhabited planets) is important to Christian ecology because no matter how far or wide or deep or small creation *is*, it remains, with all its countless galaxies and hyper-complex genomes, God's creation. And all of it is included in the 'all things' created in Christ. Just as earth spirituality includes pre-natal and terminal life, so also we include the possibility that other life may exist, has existed, or some day will exist. Openness to extraterrestrials is not necessarily – although it can be – an escape from responsibilities for our own backyards. I would argue it should be the reverse: that the possibilities of life out there should make us love our earth, especially our local bioregions, even more.

My first introduction to outer space occurred improbably when I was a boy at my grandmother's cottage on Lake Huron. My parents took me to our local farmer where they purchased eggs, chickens and fruit and vegetables every week. In the yard where the chickens ran and scratched happily, was a large roundish object looking like a chunk of ironstone. The farmer told us it was a meteorite that had landed there one night. Fragments occasionally landed around the Great Lakes, although most burned up in the outer atmosphere. But no one said anything about possible *life* out there. Only years later in high school did Jesuit religious education teachers tell us that extraterrestrial life, even rational life, could not be ruled out. Later still when I studied philosophy, and then theology, I discovered that philosophers and physical scientists are searching for signals of life in the depths of the earth, in the fossil record, and well beyond the earth.

Astronomers especially are looking far abroad. As scientists finally eliminate the moon as a living habitat, telescopes probe even further in the quest for extraterrestrial vitality. NASA plans, barring expensive terrestrial catastrophes, regularly to probe Mars, eventually recovering Martian rocks for laboratory investigation. These, with Martian fragments already found in Antarctica, may soon resolve whether or not life ever existed, lives now, or will evolve on that frigid planet. The European Space Agency anticipates launching early next century an 'Interferometry Observatory', to probe for signs of life from relatively earthlike planets. Such explorations, from both sides of the Atlantic, with continuing advances in astronomical science, the popularity of space fiction, and fascination with para-religious movements, make certain that, at least for the foreseeable future, people will wonder about extraterrestrial life, its possibilities, its remains, its evolutionary potential, and its unnoticed presence even now.

Earthlings have wondered about star folk for a surprisingly

long time. In the golden age of Greece, philosophers debated the possibilities of a plurality of worlds including planets with intelligent life. In the fifth century BC Pythagoras thought the moon, fascinating and visible from the earth then as now, was inhabited. So did Epicurus, and famously somewhat later, the prolific essayist and biographer Plutarch. Parmenides, Plato and Aristotle dismissed pluralism, or the possibility of life elsewhere. But some early church Fathers, including Clement of Rome, Irenaeus, Clement of Alexandria, Origen and Jerome, were open to possibilities of stellar life. Aquinas, like Augustine, thought this earth alone was habitable but resolutely affirmed Divine omnipotence. Three years after Aquinas' death the Bishop of Paris (Etienne Tempier) in 1277 fuelled speculation about extraterrestrials by condemning the proposition 'that the First Cause cannot make many worlds'. In other words, it is unlikely, but if God so willed, God *could* create other inhabited planets.

Since Bishop Tempier's high profiled intervention – although not necessarily *because of* it – the planetary debate has quickened. Theology, philosophy, astronomy, the physical and life sciences, literature and art have contributed, collaborated and sometimes clashed. Extraterrestrial hypotheses have included vegetative, microbial, sensate, and intelligent life. Possibilities of future evolution have been proposed – and denied. Some thinkers, not all of them believers, have dismissed the very possibility of life beyond planet earth. Some churchmen have feared – and some still fear – that a plurality of worlds with intelligent life would compromise God's unique revelation and redemption in Jesus. Philip Melanchthon, an early associate of Martin Luther, wrote, 'It must not be imagined that there are many worlds, because it must not be imagined that Christ died and was resurrected more often, nor must it be thought that in another world without the knowledge of the Son of God, that men would be restored to eternal life.'[1] In the seventeenth century the brilliant French Catholic, Blaise Pascal, seemed to fear that humans were alone in the unbroken silence of infinite space. 'Let him regard himself as lost, and from this little dungeon, in which he finds himself lodged, I mean the universe, let him learn to take the earth, its realms, its cities, its houses and himself at their proper value. What is a man in the infinite?'[2] As if to underline the plurality *of views* taken by believers, a prominent contemporary of Pascal, the friar Marin Mersenne, affirmed the possibility of extraterrestrials to be compatible with Christian faith. The silence of scripture about inhabitants of other worlds, Mersenne argued, does not mean earth's uniqueness is an article of faith. 'It seems to me that this truth must be concluded: that the statement that asserts that there are not many worlds, or what is the same, that this world of ours whose parts we see, is unique, is not concluded from the Faith.'[3] Galileo and Descartes, two important influences on European thought, were cautiously receptive of extraterrestrial hypotheses, unlike Melanchthon and Pascal. Agreement – and disagreement – about extraterrestrials makes strange roommates. Michael Crowe observes, 'Allies in a dozen conflicts, authors agreeing on a hundred issues, disagreed on extraterrestrial life. Anglicans argued against Anglicans, Catholics against Catholics, materialists against materialists.'[4]

Luminaries who favoured pluralist hypotheses included Leonardo da Vinci, Giordano Bruno, Nicholas de Cusa, Edmund Spenser, John Donne, Thomas Paine, Alexander Pope, William Wordsworth, Percy Bysshe Shelley, Lord Byron, Alfred Lord Tennyson, Daniel Bentley, Immanuel Kant, Pierre

Simon de La Place, Charles Darwin, Thomas Huxley, Gottfried Leibniz, Richard Simpson, Mark Twain and Teilhard de Chardin. The early American conservationist Henry David Thoreau, in nineteenth-century Massachusetts, illustrates a sharply different attitude towards population in outer space than that of the more lonely Pascal. 'How far apart, think you, dwell the two most distant inhabitants of yonder star? Why should I feel lonely? Is not our planet in the Milky Way?' [5] The Vatican left the extraterrestrial life question open. Indeed Pius IX's Director of the Roman College Observatory, Angelo Secchi, favoured the pluralist hypothesis, as do the Jesuit Directors of the Vatican Advanced Technology Telescope at Tucson today.

Especially since the seventeenth century, a divergence of *methodologies* between science and theology has surfaced. Theologians occasionally, and unwisely, most famously in the Galileo debacle, have trespassed beyond the limits of their own competence. More often, and no less unwisely, scientists, in what is called 'the scientific age', have transgressed the limits of their own scientific expertise, exposing themselves as virtual aliens in theological terrain. Unbelievers, including some scientists, who imagine that discoveries of life on outer planets would confound Christian faith share the same fundamentalist misunderstanding of biblical literary forms as do fundamentalist believers. In an 1867 paper the fiery unbeliever John Tyndale, then superintendent of the Royal Institute, argued that the probability of extraterrestrials made incongruous the Jewish and Christian literature. Not only did Tyndale wade beyond his theological depth, his conjectural 'countless worlds' freighted with life, despite centuries of probing outer space, remain undiscovered. Tyndale notwithstanding, the investigation continues, with believers among the explorers. Tyndale's mis-understanding of biblical literature appears when he says,

> Transferring our thoughts from this little sand-grain of
> an earth to the immeasurable heavens, where countless
> worlds with freights of life probably revolve unseen ...
> and bringing these reflections face to face with the idea
> of the Builder and sustainer of it all showing Himself in
> a burning bush, exhibiting His hinder parts, or behav-
> ing in other familiar ways ascribed to Him in Jewish
> Scripture, the Incongruity must appear.

Among pluralists there is often a tendency to assume that when conditions necessary for life are present life will evolve. Hence our generation's fascination with listening for murmurs from distant atmospheres. But necessary conditions for life are not necessarily *sufficient* conditions. Nor does the possibility of billions of galaxies make *life* even on one planet provable. Nor is the 'assumption of mediocrity' – that conditions in stellar ecosystems would be pretty much like our own – demonstrable. In this at least Pascal was precociously brilliant in his loneli-ness. The theory of evolution is not necessarily predictive. Loren Eisley argues poetically that our species will never be found elsewhere,

> Nowhere in all space or on a thousand worlds will there
> be men to share our loneliness. There may be wisdom;
> there may be power; somewhere across space great
> instruments, handled by strange, manipulative organs,
> may stare vainly at our floating cloud wrack, their
> owners yearning as we yearn. Nevertheless, in the
> nature of life and in the principles of evolution we have

had our answer. Of men elsewhere, and beyond, there
will be none forever.[6]

Some environmentalists who (understandably but mis-
takenly, I believe) dismiss the environmental wisdom of world
religions, while still working with believers who care about
God's earth, seek 'salvation' not in God but from extraterrestrials. The late Carl Sagan thought the detection of a star beat
might lead us to wisdom out there providing us with 'an
invaluable piece of knowledge: that it is possible to avoid the
dangers of the period through which we are passing.... It is
possible that among the first contents of such a message may
be detailed prescriptions for the avoidance of technological
disaster.'

Jesus and the stars

Are Melanchthon and Pascal, Tyndale and Sagan right that
Jesus does not impinge on stellar life? Are we terrestrials alone
(with God) in the universe? Or are we prospective beneficiaries
of eco-salvation through extraterrestrial wisdom? If we do have
company in the stars will these other rational beings be less
prone to self-extinction than we? These questions continue to
circulate. We owe it to our contemporaries and to tomorrow –
and, I would add, to the earth – to reflect upon them, trying to
respond as humbly and as faithfully, both to ecological restraints and to the wisdom of our tradition, as we are able.

The possibility of extraterrestrial life, in our own or in distant solar systems, is a possibility with many variables. Somewhere there may exist other beings more complex, more
intelligent, wiser and more able than we. There may be some
more prone to sin, more defiant, more ecologically abusive

than we. Or they may be more sustainable in their life styles, not fossil fuel addicted, more caring of their own kind and other beings, less prone to rebellion. Some may long ago have lived within the warmth of their suns and now be extinct, perhaps not even leaving traces for future space probes. They may not yet exist. They may be in process. They may or may not need redemption. One fact seems clear: if there ever were or are, or will be intelligences elsewhere in the universe they will be different than are we. God may have revealed and may yet reveal His love to other beings in unique ways. But only we, *homo sapiens*, have evolved here, on our small planet, possibly from one African mother. God's Word became incarnate in our flesh only here, in Judea, on our planet. What Pope Leo stated in his famous tome to Patriarch Flavian (13 June 449) happened *here*: 'Fecundity was given to the Virgin by the Holy Spirit, but the reality of the body was taken from her body; and with Wisdom building a dwelling for herself (Prov. 9.1), the Word was made flesh, and dwelt among us (Jn. 1.14); that is, in the flesh which he took from a human being and which he animated with the breath of rational life' (PL54, 762–3). Despite the possibly terminal damage our species is doing to life on earth, we may be, under God, the most complex creatures to have evolved in the universe. As C. F. D. Moule observes, 'Despite its microscopic bulk, it is conceivable that in terms of the quality of relationship, the human race represents the apex of God's creation.'[7]

When we reflect upon the time and stellar conditioned primitive preaching, we realize that when the first Christians proclaimed what God did and does in Jesus, their literal sense – what they intended and conveyed to their hearers in their preaching – was influenced by their own cosmologies. No generation, no person, including Jesus within his generation, moves beyond his generation's cosmology (its world and universe understanding). The primitive preaching does not address the possibility of a plurality of worlds with extraterrestrial life. The first Christians understood 'all things' created and redeemed in Christ within the confines of their own cosmologies. The 'principalities, dominions, and powers' above, however, are more inclusive than the first Christians realized. Jesus, God's Word, is Lord even of possible worlds which may or may not need evangelization and redemption. Jesus is truly, in Dante's final words, 'the love that moves the sun and the other stars.' Here on earth Jesus, risen from the dead, became in his humanity what he always is in his divinity, the very centre of the universe. Other planets may have good news to tell *us* about what God did for their communities. We will be able to tell them that *here*, in the midst of our community, God became a Man. In Alice Meynell's words,

> But in the eternities
> Doubtless we shall compare together, hear
> A million alien gospels, in what guise
> He trod the Pleiades, the Lyre, the Bear.
>
> Oh be prepared, my soul,
> To read the inconceivable, to scan
> The infinite forms of God those stars unroll
> when, in our turn, we show to them a Man.[8]

Loving the lonely planet

The possibility of discovering other planetary ecosystems should move us to love our earth community more not less. Our very listening for stellar echoes can help people restrain the anthroposolism (ourselves alone) which prompts people blasphemously to disregard this fragile planet where Jesus lived, died and was buried in the depths of a garden. Our listening for extraterrestrials in other ecosystems with other suns enables us to appreciate earth's biodiversity more, not less. We earthlings are beings in relationships which include God, and all that God has made and saved. Our planet includes the cross on Calvary, the grave in a garden, and the risen cosmic Christ who transcends and fills our planet and all things (Col. 1.15–20; Eph. 4.10). Our fleeting moment of life in this planet is the one moment in which we personally can *contribute to* the earth. In our local bioregions we can share and let flourish life's fecund beauty, here in our brief lifetimes we are privileged 'to pronounce judgement in uprightness of soul' (Wisd. 9.3). Every momentary lifetime is a fleeting but unique opportunity to fall upon our knees in wonder at earth's beauty and variety, and God's presence caring for us through earth's bounteous fertility and generosity. The dying playwright Dennis Potter was filled with terminal wonder at the plum tree blossoming beneath his window. I was moved to hear him say in a final interview,

> It is, and it is *now* ... and that nowness has become so vivid to me that ... I'm almost serene. I can celebrate life. Below my window ... the blossom is out in full. It's a plum tree; and instead of saying, 'Oh, that's nice blossom', looking at it through the window it is the whitest, frothiest, blossomest blossom there ever could be. And I can see it; and things are both more trivial than they ever were and more important than they ever were, and the difference between the trivial and the important doesn't seem to matter, but the nowness of everything is absolutely wondrous.

There still lived memories of the gentle passenger pigeons when I grew up in northwest Detroit. Now even the living memories of the gentle pigeons – like memories of life in the Flanders' trenches – are gone with the pigeons. The pigeons did not go alone. Men also shot for pleasure the black bears and grizzlies, the gentle moose and forest buffalo and the dwarf caribou. God will never again communicate with men through a passenger pigeon or a dwarf caribou. Men can make extinct the voices of God. Further west on the Pacific coast there used to be 100,000 Spring run Chinook salmon in Californian rivers. The salmon are commercially extinct now, battered and polluted not just by cruelty and greed, but by a lack of love and wonder by millions of guilty bystanders who would never spear a salmon or shoot a pigeon.

For every person who cares about plums and pigeons and salmon there are others like those described in William Blake's famous line, 'The tree which moves some to tears of joy is in the eyes of others only a green thing which stands in the way.' There are Americans who talk about colonizing planets and 'terraforming' Mars, with atomic explosions if necessary, and then moving on to other Jamestowns. Why worry about this disposable planet when there is always a new one parked just outside? With all respect to Texas 'can do', it seems rather rash even with American technology, to expect NASA to transport six billion people into outer space. And even if there are gaias out there, their presence or possibility is no reason to despoil the plums and birds and sea creatures of this small planet. An American statesman, wiser and more attuned to the prairies than many succeeding Republicans, left a nugget of wisdom to us. 'With public sentiment nothing can fail, without it nothing can succeed', Abraham Lincoln said. We, Christ's followers, are 'the public', God's people baptized into Jesus, God's creating and sustaining Word. We, Christ's followers, include but extend beyond our clergy who represent us and, for weal or woe, reflect us from whom they come. Whether or not we despoil or heal our planet depends upon ourselves and not just the clergy. Whether our ministers lead, or later affirm our healing actions, the responsibility for God's earth belongs to all of us who are the public. We, as Christians, have met the Church and it is us. If we, God's pilgrim people, do not cherish God's image within ourselves, if we do not love ourselves and all pre-natal and terminal and damaged human life, we will hardly love the flame in each and every creature God has made. Nor can we love even our fellow people if we do not love the world into which every person comes. Our fellow creatures are, under God, each in their distinctiveness, bearers of the divine flame. Anyone who has lived with pekes knows that each peke is a unique personality. Other creatures too are individuals. As priestly sovereigns, in this frail planet and not on any other, it is our responsibility to let each being, in the locality where we live, be what he or she or it is. Our ministry is to enable them to say – to us, to one another, and to God – what they are. In Gerard Manley Hopkin's words,

> Each mortal thing does one thing and the same:
> Deals out that being indoors each one dwells;
> Selves – goes itself; *myself* it speaks and spells,
> Crying *What I do is me: for that I came.*[9]

To empower plums and pigeons and salmon, to let them be what they are, is to accompany them to eternity. Our mission in life is, in brief, to liturgize the cosmos. To appreciate God's image in ourselves – and therefore in the earth – leading earth creatures to eternity, demands that sacrifice which is inherent to being, in Christ, God's people. Sacrifice, more than 'giving up', means making holy, giving thanks, and transfiguring the earth community into a eucharistic community of praise, as in the western liturgies when we say, 'all creation rightly gives you praise.'

Conclusion

Beyond our planet there may exist a plurality of worlds, whole thinking kingdoms, some with lives of unsuspected shapes and forms and complexities. The possibility of strangers out there, of aliens to us, should be for us not a source of anxiety, much less of earth abuse, but of wonder at what God has done for ourselves and our earth in Jesus. Jesus, God's personal Wisdom incarnate, fills all worlds of life wherever they may be. Our mission is to transfigure the galaxies and to lead the cosmos in praise and thanksgiving, not by dreams of terraforming elsewhere, but by healing, conserving, transforming and cherishing our own small planet in the locality, the neighbourhood, where we live.

CHAPTER EIGHT

Earth Spirituality in Diaspora

We still do not *know* any more than did Plutarch or Descartes whether or not there are thinking beings elsewhere in the universe. But we are learning how large the universe is – and how fragile and complex is life here on our own small planet. It is *here* on earth, especially in our own neighbourhoods, that we respond to Holy Mystery, especially present in Jesus risen, in our earth. While telescopes stretch and probe ever further abroad, satellites in space report what is actually happening *here* where we find God, on our earth. Relentlessly they expose what the Orthodox theologian Philip Sherrard describes as,

> our present path of devastation in a kind of blindfold nightmare enacted with all the inevitability of a Greek tragedy, planning to extend our empire of sterilized artificiality and specialist methodology even further, advancing even further into the computerized or electronic wilderness, devising bigger and better banking systems, manipulating the natural reproductive processes of plants, animals and human beings, saturating our soils and crops with high-powered chemicals and a variety of poisons which no sane community would

allow out of a closely-guarded laboratory, stripping the world of what is left of its forests at a speed which defies belief or understanding, and behaving generally in a manner which, even if we had deliberately programmed it, could not be more propitious to our own annihilation and to that of the world about us.[1]

This is our world where we meet God. Even if we wished to hide from the realities revealed by the satellites and by environmentalists, even if we wanted to escape from God's grace and demands, we could not. There is no sanctuary planet elsewhere, with or without life, nor is there a secret garden on this one, where we could hide from God who knows us. Spiritual writers, I think especially now of Bernard Bassett and Thomas Merton, describe how we are actors, we play a part before fellow creatures even when we pray. But we cannot avoid God's loving glance. Merton, who, after two decades of communal Trappist life, ended his monastic days as a hermit in his own cottage in the Kentucky hills, observed that sham is pointless in solitude. Alone with God who touches us in our inmost thoughts the solitary knows that he is known, that even if he wanted to hide, or to act a part, he is known. Spirituality is about truth. Our hermitage, our place of solitude with Holy Mystery, is our planet especially in the place where we live. Here in our global hermitage we want to acknowledge the truth as solitaries face it. With God we want to be our true selves and to be loved. The truth is that our contemporaries now engaged in consumer capitalism are destroying the earth, that consumer lifestyles and aspirations and widespread family disintegration endanger the future. Moreover, especially since the Rio Earth Summit of 1992 we know what we are doing. Immediately after the summit the mass media returned to reporting trivia as usual. But they were too late. Since June 1992 and the subsequent events that followed that (in retrospect) climatic gathering, *people know*.

In the years immediately before Rio I met, over an eighteen-month period, with Christians of different traditions in consultations at St George's House, Windsor Castle, on the Christian attitude to nature. Most of us shared the then received view that if people were alerted to what treadmill industrialism was doing to the earth and the future, 'the better angels of our nature' would move us to healing and sustainability, that especially for the children we would secure what the 1987 Brundtland Report called 'our common future'. Environmentalists, educators, and eminent scientists, therefore, launched an impressive educational crusade to 'make people more aware'. Many joined the effort: representatives from industry, government, local authorities, environmental journalists, educators, celebrities, European royalty, religious leaders, culminating in concerted television exposure and the Earth Summit itself. In a way this admirable massive effort succeeded. It prepared soil and souls for the penny which dropped at Rio. It shook the shallow, disturbed the comfortable, and informed old and young.

But it failed to change the world. It failed because, before Rio, *we* failed to realize that the problem is less of the head than of the heart. Our fault lies not with our satellites or telescopes, but with our imagery, our love, our caring about our fellow creatures where we live. All of us are like solitaries in our hermitage. We are too well informed about ourselves and the earth to hide within clouds of unknowing, we cannot even muster supine (reality avoiding) ignorance. We suffer from affective heart disease. We have difficulty responding to God's gift of himself in his creatures. Which is to say we have ecological heart failure.

Where do we go from here?

How do we pray, serve God and heal the earth in such an affectively dysfunctional world? For an earth spirituality for the future we may say that to get to Tipperary we would prefer not to start from here. I do not think spiritualities of human sexuality and transpersonal subjectivity respond adequately to God in the earth. We can begin, however, by purifying our feelings about our bodies and *ourselves*. How we regard our embodied selves determines in a major way how we feel about the whole earth community. If we regard ourselves – as millions are taught to do – as pleasure-oriented bipeds in a shoppers' mall world, then we may regard our earth not as a community in need of love and healing, a community of subjects with which we are forever related, but as a transient apple, a vast, dwindling resource for our species to mine, exploit, genetically engineer, cover with concrete, and discard.

Our own earth spirituality is reflected in the way we educate our children. Do we try to sensitize them to the earth community and their place within it, especially around their homes and neighbourhoods? Do we educate whole persons in our schools? If we regard the earth merely as a consumption resource we will not 'lead forth' whole persons in our schools, we will not promote ecological religious education, we will not teach service to other people and to the whole earth community. We will not teach them their own history, the classics, the fine arts, geology. Rather we will be – and we are – training youngsters for employability, 'getting ahead', doing well, in 'an increasingly competitive' consumer wonderworld, specialists in choice, marketing, e-mail, information technology, and shopping.

Where on earth is God found?

At the origins of a distinctively Christian earth spirituality Paul and Barnabas told the Lystrians, 'He did not leave himself without witness, for he did good and gave you from heaven rains and fruitful seasons' (Acts 14.17). For these first missionaries, Holy Mystery, especially present in Jesus, is also immanent in the gifts of the fruitful earth. God discloses himself in what later Christians call 'the two books': the natural world and his Word in the Bible. Humility and reticence before Mystery has been a theme of this book. We encounter God in the natural world quietly and always in mystery. When tempted to talk too much about *what* God is, we need to reinhabit our apophatic, quiet, reverent tradition about God in nature and in Jesus. The two books are best read on our knees in the silence of the earth's cloister. William of St Thierry, the medieval Benedictine abbot who later became a Cistercian, when visiting the abbey of Clairvaux, said that when the monks were not at work in the fields the only sounds in the wooded valley were of the choir monks singing, the only teachers the oaks and beeches. I have listened in the forest of Clairvaux near the ever flowing springs that once served the choir monks and lay brothers, and there in the silence the oaks and beeches still teach the presence of Holy Mystery in our earth.

The God who reaches out to us in the birds and oaks and beeches, in the springs and people near us, is uniquely present in Jewish history culminating in Jesus. The 'second book', the Bible, testifies to Jesus. We discover the triune God not as 'data' but shining in the face of Jesus Christ. No matter how evolutionary, vast or chaotic scientists discover our universe to be, we behold ultimate Mystery and Peace in the earth community and in Jesus. Our mission and ministry is sublime, unique within the earth community, it is to respond in love and service to God present in the earth and in Jesus, and to facilitate the praise of God by children, birds, oaks and beeches. The whole earth, as William of St Thierry realized at Clairvaux, is a community of praise within which we offer Jesus crucified and risen, reconciling all things to the Father in the living Spirit. But we who are God's image, priestly sovereigns under God, remain *within* the earth community in whose company we pray. We err, when we presume to say more about Holy Mystery than Jesus did when he addressed God as Abba, Father, among the silent trees of Gethsemane. The Anglican priest poet George Herbert (d. 1633) elevates humanity unduly when he writes,

> Man is the world's High Priest: he doth present
> The sacrifice for all: while they below
> Unto the service mutter an assent.

Herbert is right that humans are priestly sovereigns under God offering the earth community's praise to the Father, wrong that our fellow creatures are below or that they only mutter an assent. The birds and springs, oaks and beeches praise God in their distinctive ways. We and our fellow creatures remain covenant partners who together praise God while awaiting final transformation (Gen. 9.9–10; Rom. 8.19–23).

Christianity and nature in diaspora

Christians, at least in the west, are now a minority movement analogous to the relatively few and scattered Jewish people. We too are in diaspora with the strains, the difficulties in retaining continuity, and the partial disaffiliation that a scattered condition brings. At the same time the healthy biodiversity of the earth, for which we are responsible, is also scattered and shrinking. These two diaspora, of Christianity and of biodiversity, are not unrelated. For at the very time the shoppers' arcade beckons as if the earth can thrive, like a millennial dome, with religion as one of the shows, it becomes more obvious that only through earth spirituality will humanity heal and live sustainably upon the earth. At the very moment of our diaspora, the earth community needs healing as seldom before. Engagement with the earth, deep Christian earth spirituality, is today's compelling mission for the people of the Incarnation. Every wounded bush must be healed, for it is the burning bush, every mountain is holy, every stream the Jordan – his cross is every tree. The earth is our temple where we need to take off our shoes and lead the community to God who is our Father. The Orthodox theologian Vincent Rossi writes, 'We need men and women to feel religious about nature. We need "monks" and "nuns" in the temple of the earth.'

Diaspora children

The smouldering rainforests, the floods and erosion of people's homes in Central America, the relentless construction on fields and habitats at home, the increasing dominance of cars and roads, emissions and noise, planes and airports, the whole greying of the living environment, mean that our children, the diaspora children, grow up with impoverished imaginations. They rarely behold the wonders of earth's beauty. The most beautiful nature documentaries – and many *are* technically brilliant and beautiful – cannot replace the primary experience, the touch and sound and smell of fellow creatures, the opportunity to hear dawn choruses, to walk near bluebell woods, to wonder at bees pollinating plums, to enjoy the mysterious, almost personal companionship of wild animals born free. Diaspora children cannot taste what is no more. They suffer the extinction of experience. The extinction of beauty and biodiversity and of experience are related. Battery-reared children driven to school cannot experience spring catkins or breathe clean air. Like developing peoples, they are surfeited and manipulated by mass media, often by the same adverts whether on television screens at home or overseas on CNN. Developing people, surrounded by adverts, aspire to the utopian consumerism of what we call the developed world, while children in industrialized regions aspire to a little more consumption than that of their parents.

This is the diaspora context in which we struggle to relate children and people everywhere to an earth community reconciled in Jesus Christ. Unless our lived evangelization includes reduced consumption of the earth and promotes fewer aspirations for yet more consumption, neither affluent children nor aspirant people have a bright future. We are challenged to cultivate children's innate taste for living creatures, to educate whole embodied persons, encourage curiosity and wonder, instil a sense of community service of other beings and of the future. Education for 'employability' in 'the market', in 'an increasingly competitive world' is education misnamed. We need, as Rossi says, to feel religious about nature.

The political option
For young and old, spirituality, like theology, flows into practice. People committed to earth spirituality differ about the desirability of engagement in politics even on the fringes. Al Gore, who has been involved both in earth spirituality and in politics for almost his entire adult life, said, before he entered the top echelons of American politics, 'Current public

discourse is focused on the shortest of short-term values and encourages the American people to join us politicians in avoiding the most important issues and postponing the really difficult choices.'[2] Especially on urgent environmental issues politicians, encouraged by comfortable constituents and television journalists, engage in reality avoidance, trying to focus attention on minor distractions and 'the economy'. Some environmentalists, passionately committed to the healing and restoring of the earth, respond by opting out of all politics. Others, like Gore and Tim Wirth and Bruce Babbitt in the USA, John Gummer and Elliott Morley in Britain, and Trevor Sargent in Ireland, involve themselves at the political centre.

Thoughtful observers argue convincingly that in America there is only the American business party with democrat and republican branches. I would add that in the UK the party has three branches. If minority special interests alone engage seriously in politics, then profit-driven exploitation of people, the wider earth community, and the future, will continue. Therefore I believe that people committed to an earth spirituality should participate in some way in local, regional, and national politics – in that order. Each of us, committed to the earth Jesus risen from the dead, has one voice, one vote, one purse, one pen, one presence, but with these five small contributions we can make a difference.

If politics without earth spirituality rarely serves the whole *polis*, but serves minority special interests, then the contribution of believers who care about the earth is important. For a religious contribution includes the good of the whole city. The American environmentalist Max Oelschlaeger writes, 'Religious discourse, expressing itself in the democratic forum, offers the possibility of overcoming special interest politics – especially those which are narrowly economic – on environmental issues.'[3] But, Oelschlaeger adds, there is a paradox. Nearly 90 per cent of Americans claim religious affiliation, yet Americans are almost unsurpassed as world class mega-consumers. 'Americans, regardless of their faith commitments, apparently prefer to live in ways that require massive consumption of natural resources and generate high outputs of waste (pollution).'[4] Unsustainable consumption by believers, who should be not part of the problem but part of the solution, is perhaps the most serious wound in a world of wounds, because a materialistic, technological response, without an earth spirituality, cannot heal and restore the earth.

I suggest that individual Christians who care about the earth, rather than grasp at institutional survival in a diaspora situation, should contribute to earth healing in Christ the Suffering Servant. Every Eucharist is an ecological event in which we recall, memorialize and make present, God's reconciliation of the earth community in Jesus, God's suffering and glorious Servant. Jesus crucified and risen, with whom we identify in our Eucharist, restores the everlasting rainbow covenant of God with all creation. Our Christian contribution offers more than hope in a gaia evolution after our species, and our damage, disappears, a misnamed hope seriously proposed by some scientists who despair of the human spirit. Our Christian contribution, at every Eucharist, celebrates an earth spirituality which cherishes every blossom. In the words of a Benedictine prayer at Lauds and Vespers, 'Lord, all creatures are sparks from your brilliance, for there is no living thing without some kind of radiance. Help us to cherish all that you have made.'

Loving the earth

As I write, small apples, having succeeded still smaller blossoms, swell in my garden. Small apples are very much within earth spirituality. As Chesterton noted, reconciliation in Jesus includes them too,

> For our God hath blessed creation,
> Calling it good. I know
> What spirit with whom you blindly band
> Hath blessed destruction with his hand;
> Yet by God's death the stars shall stand
> And the small apples grow.
>
> – G. K. CHESTERTON
> 'The Ballad of the White Horse'

I have long wondered how a lived earth spirituality can help the earth community in its conscious members, especially our children in towns and cities, to fall in love with itself again every spring and every day. It is not enough to include 'the environment' in school curricula, in religious education, in government departments, and in industrial decisions. We have to love the earth visibly in our own lives. Only then can we stir sensitivity akin to Chesterton's love of vines and small apples, to Yeat's appreciation of 'the silver apples of the moon, the golden apples of the sun', to Teilhard's hymn to the universe,

> Blessed are you, reality every new-born; you who, by constantly shattering our mental categories, force us to go ever further and further in our pursuit of the truth; triple abyss of stars and atoms and generations: you who by overflowing and dissolving our narrow standards of measurement reveal to us the dimensions of God.[5]

We need an earth spirituality which enables us to feel religious kinship with the earth. Deacon Jean-Pierre Ribault, President of the European Francis of Assisi Academy, observes that people in the European Community will not live sustainably until we learn to *love* and appreciate and respect nature 'in its entirety' – our small apples again, 'We will be unable to save our natural surroundings until we learn to appreciate a sunset over a reedy marsh or the black redstart's first song announcing sunrise, in short, until we really love nature, until we respect it in its entirety.'

The key to a genuinely sustainable future, to what John Seymour calls 'the real new age, the age of healing', is living sustainably *where we are*, in our own neighbourhoods, in our bioregions. We can think and act globally and locally by taking responsibility for the welfare of our own local habitats where we live. As the late Tip O'Neill said, 'all politics is local'. So is sustainability. Every house plant, window box, small bird, apple tree, compost bin, in our neighbourhood, is supremely important for the whole earth now and for the future. The words 'ecology' and 'environment' remain useful, providing we include the whole earth community in our ecology and environment. We are other creatures' environment – and they are ours. The UN Security Council cannot preserve local countryside or urban sites from the greed of predatory developers and the insensitivity of politicians and planners, but local councillors, supported by many of us, can make a difference.

Every neighbourhood and every town, like every garden, is distinct and unique. Getting to know one's local soils, flora and fauna, seasonal migrants, and local food and drink in its distinctiveness, is one of the pleasures of a lifetime. We need to appreciate again the ways and riches of our local bioregions as the medieval Cistercians and French countrymen appreciated theirs. Wine and apples, milk and cheese, even the taste of vegetables can vary from field to field, or allotment or garden. *Vignerons* in the Burgundy *côtes* can distinguish wine from different corners of the same vineyard. Some English pomologists can compare the taste of apples or cider from one year (or vintage) to the next depending on the autumn sun. Urban allotment subculture shares lore, crops and seed, a sharing that comes with learning the different ways of local soil, a learning which never ceases. Edible landscapes – decorative food plants – in gardens and public spaces delight both eye and taste – and vary from town to town and even within a town. Urban fruit growing is in its infancy with a potential to please and feed city people and wildlife while contributing to a pleasant environment. Street names like 'Orchard Close' can take on more than nostalgic meaning. Even woodland burials near settlements remind us that we are earthlings within an earth community which, in death, we reinhabit in a pancosmic way, more pervasively united to the earth than before. In the new creation, as in this life, we share a common future with the whole earth. As the late Raymond Brown used to say, 'In Jesus risen the earth shares our future. We should take care of it'.

Earth healing

We live in an earth of wounds. Earth spirituality includes healing. People cannot be healed apart from the whole earth. Whole habitats and species have been almost terminally damaged, even extinguished by human conduct. Conservationists do well to remember that before we can *conserve* we need to restore. Before we can preserve what life and species remain, we need to heal the damage done and still being done as, for example, in deforestation in the Americas, in militarism everywhere, and in the visible degradation of our own neighbourhoods. Complacent and comfortable people, who have difficulty relating to the natural world, argue that to talk about earth healing is to contradict twentieth-century progress, that to translate 'conservation' into radical healing and restoration is 'going back'.

In fact ecological, holistic healing of God's earth community is going back – to biodiversity, flourishing habitats in town and country, clear air and water, and closeness of people to nature. Earth healing returns to planting and managing hedgerows again, to woodlands and open spaces in towns and cities, rural and urban wildlife habitats, clean rivers and beaches, fields and hills, and sustainable shared transport. Earth healing requires going back to quiet, leafy neighbourhoods, undominated by traffic, to organic growing of food and other plants, where children walk safely to school again, to sharing and compassion for those in need, solidarity with those less fortunate than the majority, less able, lonely, and with those who are disturbed. Earth healing includes a return to stable family life where children, the elderly and neighbours are loved, where love is not rationed to 'quality time'.

Earth *abuse* is a grave structural evil requiring repentance by all of us. Restitution for the injustice of earth abuse, injustice to the whole earth community, means, for example, that we literally must remove some pavement and roll back asphalt with which for decades we have crushed the earth. Rolling back asphalt lets life regenerate where there is death. Each of us in our neighbourhoods can heal the sorry 'state we are in' by removing some slabs, concrete or pavement from near our homes, churches, offices, and schools, letting life live again. For many of us this means we can perhaps remove an inch, others can lift whole slabs, still others can help to reforest military airfields and automobile graveyards.

Local healing is global healing. Our ponds, lakes, rivers and seas are precious, life nurturing havens for people and wildlife. We can let our rivers and seaside habitats flourish again. Every river restored affects all the rivers in the world, it can symbolize that we are people of the Jordan. Unnecessary upland drainage which prevents retention and causes winter floods should be removed, another 'going back' which is healing. In urban areas the removal of garden slabs and concrete enables rain to infiltrate aquifers again. We heal by supporting local organic growers and sustainable fishing, and by improved sewage treatment even when it costs. Water, as the Bible repeatedly and poetically testifies, is God's life giving gift to the whole earth community. Perhaps our common water and public transport, where broken up and privatized, should be returned to common stewardship again.[6]

Is sustainable development sustainable?

We noted that most people now know that our present behaviour is unsustainable. This knowledge is a problem for people committed to creation and incarnation in Jesus and to our common future in Jesus risen. Those of us prepared to integrate the earth into our spirituality are not always convinced that 'sustainable development' is the solution to the damage done and still being done by consumer cultures. If we must *heal* even before we can *conserve*, it does seem questionable that we can push ahead with more *development*, even if called sustainable, unless that 'development' includes healing and conservation. Since the publication of *Our Common Future* – the Brundtland Report – in 1987, the slogan 'sustainable development' has become an almost unquestioned presupposition of our culture. Sustainable development is described as development which 'meets the needs of the present without compromising the ability of future generations to meet their own needs.'[7] Unfortunately, actions and proposals, no matter how damaging to the earth, are received as above criticism on environmental grounds if they are described as sustainable development. I said sustainable development has become *almost* unquestioned. Almost but not quite. Counter-cultural voices – and they are increasing – question the recently received wisdom of sustainable development as 'a political fudge'.[8]

Questions are asked about some assumptions of sustainable development. Present and future needs of whom? generations of what? whose future? Is sustainable development merely a techno-political version of the Aristotelian view that beings which do not reason are for human use and disposal? The idea of sustainable development can easily be hijacked by economism as a slogan for the sustainability of *development* but not the welfare of the whole earth community and the future. Sustainable development is sometimes used to legitimate relentless economic growth.

Sustainable development can be divided helpfully into four readily recognizable categories. First, treadmill sustainable development promotes western growth economism everywhere, regardless of social and environmental restraints. Second, weak sustainable development continues pretty much along the primrose path of western utopian industrialism and *laissez faire*, but with some token efforts to mitigate environmental damage. Third, strong sustainable development, while not prepared to sacrifice enough for genuine sustainability, nevertheless tries to correlate industrialism with some sound ecological principles. Finally, *ideal* sustainable development is not really *development* at all, but a sustainable way of living within the earth's restraints which provides what is *sufficient* for human needs and the needs of other creatures, while securing the future of the whole earth community.[9]

Sustainable sufficiency

People ask what sustainable sufficiency in practice *means*, and how sustainable sufficiency can be integrated into earth spirituality. Response to these good questions would be almost as varied as are individuals and families and communities. Sustainable sufficiency for all of us would mean, at a minimum, living as locally (or bioregionally) as possible, taking from earth's gifts what is sufficient for ourselves and our dependants, human and non-human, while healing and conserving the whole earth community for future generations of people and all other creatures. Sustainable sufficiency is counter-cultural: living in a renewable, organic, reticent, respectful, and celebratory way within the earth's restraints. Sustainable sufficiency, as counter-cultural, sharply challenges some received wisdoms in 'developed' cultures, including the infinite resource illusions of some religious and environmental spokespeople. In sustainable sufficiency people try to live locally while thinking globally about the welfare of everyone on earth and of the future. Sustainable sufficiency presupposes that the way we live in our own locality affects every other locality. If nothing else has, the climate change crisis alone proves global interdependence. People who live – or try to live – in sustainable sufficiency cannot immediately convert the world. The important thing is not to be overwhelmed by the juggernaut of globalization, but openly to seek and discern God's will for one's self and family where we live. Neither we nor even valiant non-government organizations, to some of which we belong, can immediately, perhaps not even in our lifetimes, reverse fossil fuel and soil devouring globalization. We can however light a small candle by living locally with what is sufficient while assisting neighbours, local authorities, non-governmental organizations, and businesses in our localities who struggle to assist society towards sustainability. When we nurture a small garden, people will ask (perhaps silently) what difference it makes. It surely makes a difference to the countless organisms large and small in our small garden – and therefore to the universe. Edward Goldsmith provides food for thought,

> Today's policy is to create a global economy totally controlled by vast, uncontrollable, and irresponsible transnational corporations catering for the world market. We must instead create a network of loosely connected local economies, largely in the hands of small and medium companies that are integral parts of local communities and societies, and for whose welfare they feel deeply responsible.... It is only in this way too that we can conceivably provide people with jobs or other means of assuring their livelihood, for it is the small and medium companies that provide the bulk of available jobs, the transnationals – in spite of all their hype – providing but an insignificant proportion of those that are today available. What is more, it is also only in this way that we can create the economic infrastructure for renewed families and communities which the global economy cannot conceivably do.[10]

This means we need to influence, if in no other way at least by example, such organizations as the World Bank, the International Monetary Fund, the World Trade Organization, the European Union, the North American Free Trade Association, and the United States Congress. We cannot ignore the environmental degradation of militarism, arms races, nuclear explosions, incautious genetic engineering, ethnic cleansing, and disruptive migrations. Some transnational companies are beginning to recognize the imperative for change and are listening to responsible environmental organizations. The fundamental problem facing alternative groups now in dialogue with some of the Big Movers is the (now familiar) one of the head and the heart. And this is where earth spirituality is incalculably important. Green forums, such as Forum for the Future, can and do *teach* important people how perilous is the state we are in, they even teach people how to live. The further challenge, however, is to move them *to love*. The bottom line for *all* of us, the place for us to begin, the way we can help, is *at home* with an earth spirituality which includes sustainably sufficient practice.

CHAPTER NINE

Into the Sufficient Future:
Earth Spirituality in the Midst

In an organic garden are the seeds of an earth spirituality. I like to do theology in my raised beds as well as in my study. Other earth theologians do theology effectively elsewhere, as in parks, in the trenches, even in jail. Teilhard went from Hastings to the trenches, Yves Congar spent time in Colditz, and Dietrich Bonhoeffer is remembered for his letters and papers from prison and his martyrdom at Flossenberg. To theologize beyond one's study is not to dilute theology. Theology and spirituality close to the soil liberate theology by grounding it in the midst of the earth community. Theology needs liberation from talking to itself, from what may be called intrinsicism, it needs a preferential option for its own liberation. Which is not to suggest that earth theology can be done well apart from other theologians and from people engaged in an earth spirituality. Some of my most durable insights into God and the sacredness of the earth in Jesus risen, were gathered not in isolation but over tankards with scholars interested in spirituality in Jesuit *haustus* rooms, the common rooms where drinks are shared in Jesuit houses. Over regional beers in many *haustus* rooms I learned a lot about what Athens has to say to Manresa. I also discussed, with learned men, what a Christian earth spirituality has to offer a culture described by Beth Burrows of the Edmonds Institute, as one where, 'it is not so much that the sacred is absent. It is simply not noticed. Put another way, it may seem non-existent because it is rarely looked for. Unseen and unreported, the sacred is nevertheless still here.'[1]

To help people recover the sacredness of the earth, I am not suggesting that all theologians should be organic gardeners, environmental campaigners, or prisoners. They should however be in contact with the soil, at least in their favourite parks, and, where possible, they should tend some fruit trees, and contribute theologically and practically to alternative prophetic movements that are the only hope of bringing shalom, total integral peace, to the whole earth community, in which Holy Mystery is present and living. Theology, a Yale Divinity School lecturer once said, is the analytical mind's contribution to the praise of God. I would add that if the mind is embodied the analysis will flow into healing practice.

Liberated earth theology, if it is effectively to serve the whole earth community in Christ Jesus, must continuously reinterpret God's cosmic action in Jesus for our own changing times and questions. All God's people in Christ reinterpret Jesus for today with the help of theologians. People continually discern their theologians. Earth theology must ring true, theologians must put their spirituality and lifestyle where their words are. Earth theologians too will make mistakes and miss points. Uninvolved academics have no monopoly on finitude. Criticism from both right and left may mean that our theology is not too far from the extreme centre where truth circulates. Yet, criticism whether from the establishment or from the New Age, means that one has things to learn and a way to go. A former diocesan priest, now ministering in a quiet way in a rural parish, told me he considered himself 'a shepherd in the midst'. There are also earth theologians – including non-canonical Jesuits – in the midst. I remain in partial communion, in a mutual recognition of ministries as it were, with academic theologians, but in communion not absorption.

The midst where I have done theology, and attempted to live an earth spirituality, has been in North Yorkshire, and in East Sussex on the south coast where I remain. I appreciate and, in a way, still live in both cultures, as polydiverse as their climates and biosystems, which in turn impact the cultures. I have lectured over the years in theological colleges and universities and at conferences across Great Britain from Scotland to Wales to Kent and across the choppy Celtic Sea in Ireland. Gradually I have relinquished membership of American theological societies to which I long belonged. I still lecture occasionally in secondary schools, including grammar, comprehensive, public and state schools. I have taught in summer schools, at Southampton University, at the Vacation Term for Biblical Study at St Anne's College, Oxford, and in the English Jesuit 'Living Theology'. I have addressed, among others, the Catholic Theological Association of Great Britain, the Society of Christian Ethics at Oxford, the Adult Religious Education National Association at Dublin, the National Conference of Priests in Birmingham and the 'Christian Attitude to Nature' consultations at St George's House, Windsor Castle. I still attend lectures and conferences as a learner where I meet working theologians. If, as Norman St John Stevas said at Cambridge, an educational community is like a mountain with some ascending and others coming down, I meet many at theology conferences on the way up, fewer descending. Pressures to impress, to get a post or promotion, sometimes interfere with exchange on the footpaths. But there remain opportunities for those heading in both directions to learn from each other. At conferences one discovers where in the British Isles people are at work with similar interests. Bioregional exchange is vital for people integrating theology – and spirituality – with the earth. Unlike past years I now meet some on the way up interested in ecological theology. It is wonderful sharing their dreams and ambitions as they move forward from past battles lost and won. I still write for a spread of periodicals although most of my writing is now in the British Isles and only occasionally in North America. Formerly the proportion was the reverse. I still contribute to theological journals but more often to periodicals read by theologically interested people as well as professional theologians. I contribute occasionally to gardening magazines and to the alternative press, where some important issues are discussed in more depth than in Fleet Street religious journalism. The alternative press gets to places where other spiritualities don't reach.

Yorkshire

I once thought that for partial self sufficiency people should move to a small holding or to a village house with ample garden. This is true for people with manual dexterity and efficient public transport. Unfortunately some of us lack the former, and in Great Britain public transport is on life support fixes after decades of neglect and privatization. Paradoxically people can be more car dependent in country than in town for everything from chemist to library. Rural parents run a petrol guzzling taxi service for sedentary emperors. So Barbara, our pekes and I have settled on the edge of towns, in suburban missionary territory with access to town centre and countryside. In a suburban house and garden we can live relatively sustainably in partial self sufficiency.

We first settled in a three-bedroomed semi on the edge of the Cathedral and market town of Ripon in North Yorkshire. The Cathedral is a prayer in vernacular stone. The market brings local produce within walking distance twice a week. The house with its shared wall was energy conservative. We insulated out-side walls, loft and pipes, and added thick carpeting. We maxi-mized solar heat through windows, used an open fire and, when necessary in winter, central heating. With the insulation our fuel bills were slight. The garden was average size for 1930 semis, roughly thirty-feet wide and a hundred feet from front to rear including house and a small garage. I increased its size by having a local craftsman saw through a metre width of asphalt along the house and drive. He went through the asphalt in minutes with saw screeching and dust rising, rolled the asphalt up like a hard carpet, and carted it away where, sadly, it was probably not reused but land filled. There was an amusing feature in the garden, which neighbours called 'the Berlin Wall'. Apparently children from previous occupants of our semi annoyed neighbours on the other side. So the neighbours built a cinderblock wall about ten feet high on the boundary. We moved in about the same time as a retired farmer couple moved next door. All of us agreed that since the wall was *there*, we might as well leave it, and utilize it, unlike my asphalt. The farmers permitted us to drill holes and insert plugs for cordons. So I grew five apples and four pear cordons and a fan trained cherry thanks to the inherited Berlin Wall. Each summer fruit blossom and then fruit adorned the boundary.

We gardened organically utilizing every viable corner. Our soil was the most porous we have ever had. Behind us was a large field which had been quarried for gravel, then land filled, and is now grazed. So on the edge of a gravel quarry our soil devoured organic matter and, in the slightest drought, demanded water around fruit and vegetables. Sand tolerant crops did well, including carrots, beets, beans, potatoes, leeks, onions, brassicas, tomatoes, courgettes, and salads. There was no fruit when we arrived. I planted thirteen top fruit and, utilising walls and fences, sixteen soft fruit. Gooseberries and blackcurrants did not succeed with the porous soil, but red and white currants, and Worcesterberries, and the blackberry and raspberry families did well. I purchased over thirty fruits from R. V. Roger of Pickering. Roger has an outstanding collection of rare gooseberry varieties which generally do well in Yorkshire. I regretted I could not grow some on my porous soil. But the advice of countrymen was sound, 'Ye shouldn't fight yer soil.' So I grew what did well including a Purple Pershore plum tolerant of some east winds.

Warned by the recurrent dry summers and other climate change signals we installed a water butt, reminding me of my grandmother's barrel around which I played as a toddler on Lake Huron. My grandmother's was timeless oak which echoed when small boys kicked its weathered sides. Our Yorkshire barrel – purchased from the RSPB – was recycled plastic, another compromise in our fossil draining society. My grandmother's barrel was solely for *rain*. We erred by mingling grey water from bath and basin with our rain. We could use grey water with its soap and shampoo only on fruit and on fallow soil, and not on vegetables or in a pond. Barbara dug a small pond following instructions from gardeners' manuals. The pond soon hosted a variety of wildlife, including frogs which befriend organic growing by eating slugs. I did not have a greenhouse, preferring a cold frame which can be brought inside in winter without permanently covering the land. Most years I discovered a happy frog in my cold frame which was watered daily. The frame hosted cucumbers with large leaves, and slugs attracted by the water, the leaves and the gherkins. Coldframe frogs, in summer, have it made. What could be finer than moisture, a place to hide, and a diet of slugs? Frogs also like brassica beds, in other words wherever there is moisture, slugs and a place to hide. I kept two compost heaps on the go, topping them up with organic litter collected on rural walks or on the pavement. Well rotted compost keeps the local soil community alive and well. Once during an interview on Yorkshire television I said, 'We can survive without diamonds but not without dung.' The editor naughtily spliced that sentence onto the end of the interview. I could hardly complain because the aphorism is true. And there's a lot of earth theology there.

I belong to Heritage Seed Savers, within the HDRA, the UK's National Organic Gardening Organization. Heritage Seed Savers preserve endangered vegetable varieties which cannot be sold in the EU. They can however be traded or given away. Some (true) stories of the bureaucrats' ignorance of seeds, such as not knowing the difference between a kilogram of lettuce seeds and the same weight in potato seeds, are uniquely humorous. I saved seeds of a Victorian Cornish lettuce which overwinters and bursts into growth at the first light of spring providing the Victorians with early salads. I sent the saved seeds to the heritage 'Seed Library'. I doubt if the Cornish lettuce had been grown that far north before. It suffered during hard frosts, so I put plastic bottle cloches over each lettuce. Some winters the cloches were snowballed for days, at other times covered with ice. I removed the cloches in late February because the lettuces also suffer from excessive warmth. I saved lettuce because there was no wild lettuce around which could cross pollinate. The field behind, alas, was doused with chemicals, which fed the rye grass which stifled other plants. But I had to be careful not to let my own lettuce varieties bolt. Cross pollination could dilute the pure strain of the Cornish lettuce.

Harvest time, roughly from July through October, we call cornucopia or abundance time. But there is also the rest of the year. The shadows become noticeable even in August as nights lengthen. We neither clamped (buried) food nor ran a large freezer. We stored potatoes, onions and some carrots in the cool garage. Barbara quickly filled our small ozone friendly freezer with broad and runner beans, peas and raspberries as they matured. There was little room left for later soft fruit, including wild blackberries. Barbara began a rum pot with local strawberries and quickly filled it with a wide variety of fruit, setting it aside for long winter nights, when local fresh fruit was scarce. We've collected in jumble sales – and been given – kilner jars which, like the freezer and rum pot, quickly fill. Blackcurrants, plums and gooseberries kilner better than they freeze. So do our surplus tomatoes, cucumbers and, occasionally, local cherries. Nothing illustrates better than harvest that even people with gardens can be only *partially* self sufficient. John Seymour told me that if he were writing it again he would not describe his pace-setting book as a *complete* guide to self sufficiency. In his late years John described the ideal as *partial* self sufficiency. Barbara also made jams and preserved shallots, beet, tomato and marrow chutneys and, a favourite with guests, bread and butter pickles from a recipe my mother sent Barbara shortly before her death. Some years she preserved whole crab apples or pears. Redcurrants are a special case. We always grew a few because they do well in shade even in yards and against dark walls. Redcurrants have potential for urban fruit growing. With different varieties, planted in different light, redcurrants last for about three weeks. Unfortunately blackbirds also know about them and buzz my garden weeks before ripening time in late June. So, more than other fruit, redcurrants have to be carefully netted. They do not preserve well except for jelly and wine but are delicious eaten raw. So for three weeks we feasted like French countrymen on red and white currants. We went through most of our own fruit including apples quickly, so we supplemented our own by visiting a local PYO farm and bought some local fruit from farmers. We used bioregional fruit even in the lean days of late winter and early spring. Imported fruit is a major petrol guzzler of the food miles miasma.[2]

Fell walking is one of the perks of Yorkshire life. From our house we could walk to the high altar of Fountains Abbey in about an hour. We walked in the other direction, along the Skell, to our medieval Cathedral in ten minutes. Walking to both sites was like walking into prayer. Bernard of Clairvaux still looks down from Abbot Huby's tower at Fountains saying, as he did to young Henry Murdac of York in the twelfth century, 'Learn from one who has experienced it, thou wilt find among the woods what thou didst never find in books. Stones and trees will teach thee a lesson thou didst never hear from the masters in the schools.' The Cathedral is wise too. There are three green men there spanning the centuries. Not only is the earth a temple with mountain spires, the earth has medieval cathedrals, prayers in stone.

Public transport in Yorkshire is poor. There was once an excellent station at Ripon from which people could go all over the island including short day trips to nearby markets. In the ecologically arrogant sixties, Dr Beeching, Chairman of the British Railways Board, closed the railway to passengers in 1967, to freight in 1969. In 1970 engineers blew up the bridge over the Ure. From contemporary accounts – and more sadly even today – local people thought demolition of the railway, like the later bypass with its infilling through green fields, was progress. The nearest major station now is at York. We drove there to board trains for longer trips. We enjoyed a variety of accessible short breaks from Ripon, including breaks in the Lakes, the North York Moors, Lindisfarne, the North Sea, Whitby and the upper Dales. One does not have to travel far to be in a very different biosystem and culture.

We supported established local organizations, including the Friends of Ripon Cathedral, the Civic Society, the Yorkshire Wildlife Trust, Wensleydale Railway Association, and the conservation groups in Harrogate District. We did guided tours for school groups in the Cathedral and for the National Trust at Fountains Abbey. When the wind whistled through Skelldale, I would begin my tour, wearing a deerstalker, by apologizing for my West Riding accent! Bemused people wondered – and some asked – what a midwest twang was doing at Fountains Abbey. Others asked how I had almost inside knowledge of religious life when Fountains had been closed for 400 years. I did have a rather uncommon perspective, because Ignatius Loyola had adopted some features of the Cistercian *Carta Caritatis* when he wrote the Constitutions which guided me as a Jesuit. The tourists were right. I did feel affinity with the ghosts of the white monks in the wise and wounded stones of Fountains. Once I guided thirty Japanese who spoke almost no English. We managed somehow, largely because Bernard's stones and trees still teach.

We co-ordinated a local Christian Ecology Group which met quarterly in our lounge. We soon had over thirty supporters who shared information and encouragement and who networked among themselves. A few came from far up in the Dales, others from York. We began and ended meetings with prayer which seemed the most important ingredient for some. Few parish or circuit clergy in the eighties were attuned to earth spirituality. Now clergy are integrating creation with their ministry, and even join Christian Ecology Link. For six autumns the Ripon CEG sponsored 'Creation In Autumn', a series of Monday evening lectures in the Cathedral hall followed by discussion and stalls including local organic vegetables. When we left Ripon in 1994 the Ripon group faded, but a daughter continues to flourish as Harrogate District Christian Ecology Link. We held theology evenings every August for a different group of people, including several clergymen, interested in theology. We distributed an article or book chapter beforehand which we discussed at our home. The interest – and the numbers attending – was so vigorous that we determined to increase the meetings whether or not we stayed in Ripon.

We also supported some campaigns. We failed to save the last fragment of the ancient Celtic and Saxon monastery site, which had once been home to Celtic monks from Melrose, including Eata and the still popular St Cuthbert, until the Synod of Whitby (664). After the Celts departed, Wilfrid founded a Saxon monastery on the Ripon site, possibly introducing the Benedictine Rule to the north, and built a stone basilica, the crypt of which remains under the present Cathedral, one of the oldest rooms in Britain. Bede's history describes the monastery. His life of Cuthbert tells about that saint's stay in Ripon. In fact it was through reading Bede in Ohio that I learned that Ripon was not just the name of a town in Wisconsin. I determined some day to stay there, little realizing how long the stay would be! Willibrord, the apostle to the Frisians and first Archbishop of Utrecht, was at Wilfrid's monastery, as was Wilfrid's biographer Eddius. We tried to preserve the site for posterity as a 'Wilfrid and Cuthbert Memorial Garden'. Our MP visited the site with us when Chris Patten, a former pupil of the Benedictines, was for a while Secretary of State for the Environment. Unfortunately, clergy had sold the land to local developers. It was the era of market forces. Chris Patten moved up and on. Planning consent was granted. The developers moved fast. The site where Cuthbert and Wilfrid prayed is now a macro-large stone house with garage and forecourt. Local developers also intended to put a superstore or leisure centre – or both – on the local magnesian limestone SSSI, parts of which had been given by a local family *in perpetuo* for the children of Ripon. We organized annual wildlife walks and children's nature games at the SSSI in June, forcing a referendum on the future of the limestone habitat. It was a close run thing. But the habitat was saved for local children. Barbara then served on a local association which encouraged sustainable use of the site. She was on the Cathedral PCC and was a lay eucharistic minister. I worshipped at the Catholic church of St Wilfrid and, when possible, at the Cathedral with Barbara.

We never considered our home in south-west Ripon our final habitat. We planned to move one final time either within Ripon or back to Barbara's native home in Sussex, where Richard of Chichester in retirement tended his fig tree. For a year we walked around both towns, finally choosing a house and garden in southern Sussex as our ultimate holding. For Barbara returning to Bexhill was like Odysseus returning to

Ithaca after two decades on a northern odyssey. But for both of us leaving Ripon was hard. The years at Whitcliffe Lane were among the best in our lives. The saying is true, 'There's no place like Yorkshire'. Thankfully we return to Ripon life and people, and Ripon's prayers in stone, every Advent.

Back to Sussex

In Bexhill we sought a final habitat which was near town centre, the sea front, and a train halt so that we could be reasonably independent of the car. We wanted a garden which would enable us to follow William Cecil's advice to 'have a little land around you' for a variety of fruit and vegetables. We wanted a house which maximized solar heat and light, with space for studies, an open fire, and a large room for meetings. Barbara, who knows her home town well, made a few trips south and soon found the house that matched our 'course description'. People thought it strange that I did not accompany her, or even view the house before moving in. Yet we both knew what we were looking for. Barbara's description, embellished by a few sketches, was enough for me. We bought the house from expatriate Celts named Stewart, from Ayrshire and Tipperary, who had lived here seventeen years. They are now neighbours and friends. A solicitor friend did the conveyance for us. He said the house was in ground that had been a girls' school then a nursing home, but, beyond that, was little touched since the ice age. Certainly I uncovered few historical traces beyond builders' rubble when I dug the garden, not even a Victorian beer bottle or horseshoe.

We brought with us our Volvo, with its catalytic converter, which we had purchased in 1990, intending to keep it for at least ten years. It was, in 1990, the most environmentally friendly car – a contradiction in terms – we could find. When we exchange it, we will again purchase the 'least worst' on the market. Like wildlife adapting to counter new threats (plants versus beetles for example) purchasers must seek out the ecologically least worst choice of the moment. We still hope that when we part with the sturdy Volvo most of its parts can be reused or recycled. We also brought our bicycles. In the seventies I cycled everywhere in Bexhill without danger. Now with parked and moving cars, vans and lorries filling roads and even pavements, cycling is dangerous. Second and third car purchase is a growth practice in the home counties. Streets and even gardens are used as car parks. We still bicycle, but with diligence and at off peak times. Any time someone is forced to walk or drive when they would prefer to bicycle or use public transport the motor lobby wins another battle. In Sussex, as in Yorkshire, they win not a few.

Decades of neglect by successive governments, culminating in privatization, almost extinguished one of the world's better rail and bus networks. These are now slowly, fitfully and expensively recovering. We enjoy a bus stop a few metres from the house, whence we sometimes bus to town centre and beyond. A train halt with shelter is about twelve minutes' walk with luggage. From our house we can entrain to Paris or Brussels in about four hours. With one or two changes we can also reach most cities in the UK. On a train passengers can eat, read and work while travelling. Pollution is relatively slight. And pekes are welcome.

Our present peke, Bertha, enjoys train, bus and ship travel. When crossing London by tube she lifts urban spirits, raises smiles and, in general, fosters community. Time and again I've seen carriages – and escalators – filled with defensively dour commuters brighten at the sight of a pretty peke tucked under my arm. This is especially true of (normally reserved) Chinese women, young girls, and anyone who has lived with a peke. The latter we spot instantly by the look in their eyes as they head our, or rather, Bertha's way. You can love them or, not knowing pekes, hate them. You might even say with T. S. Eliot, that they 'are not British dogs, but heathen Chinese'. But each is a character, a love loving little person, a furry dynasty. Often I have heard strangers, who are peke persons, say 'Once you've had one, you'd never have anything else.' The late P. G. Wodehouse, a peke person, judged people by whether or not they were 'sound on pekes'! I don't think T. S. Eliot was in his pantheon.

Though I do not recommend that all leave their father's home at eighteen, as I did, and grow 'old with wandering through hollow lands and hilly lands', I cannot deny that each time I move I learn about homes and gardens – and just moving. Soon after moving to Thornbank we insulated the loft and walls. As in Ripon we could not infill some walls. Where we could not infill we added insulation to inside walls. We added about six inches of fibre-glass to the garage ceiling beneath my room. We put underlay under the carpets. We double glazed throughout and added a glass door to the dining room opening onto the garden. A local firm installed solar tubes which heat our water about half the year, including on clear winter days, and redirect surplus heat to a radiator in my room where it is especially useful in spring and autumn because the room faces southeast. With the insulation, the radiator, and sunshine from a south window the room is now snug. When we had to replace the bathroom carpet we chose one made from recycled plastic drink bottles. The water company installed a meter. Local plumbers added a Micra shower and two rainwater butts.

Because our pipes are within the walls we cannot recycle our grey water, but we carry kitchen and, in summer, shower water to fruit trees. In winter I frequently pour kitchen water onto the grass where it reaches aquifers instead of being rushed into the English Channel. Paradoxically the Channel, into which the crowded south coast pours much of its rainwater, is dangerously high while aquifers, which are paved over even in gardens, are low. Barbara again dug a wildlife pond in the partial shade of a neighbouring oak. It soon became a minor biosystem. In dry spells it requires low alkaline rainwater (as do my two blueberries) from the water butts.

As soon as we took possession, I removed all our inherited leylandii conifers which guzzle water, sterilize soil, cast shade, destroy human (and soil) communities and, like Japanese Knotweed and grey squirrels, are human introduced intruders. Like a road enthusiast uprooting green fields, I have happily exterminated about thirty leylandii in my moves. I replace them with companionable indigenous varieties, such as holly, wild apple (*malus sylvestris*), damsons and cherry plums. These improve soil fertility and provide food for people and wildlife. They are also wind resistant. I double dug a south facing vegetable garden, lining trenches with turves, organic material, and sticks and stones for drainage. Our Thornbank soil could not be more different than Whitcliffe Lane, heavy clay instead of sandy shingle. In our first autumn I spread a variety of rotted organic materials onto the newly dug clay soil, including seaweed from the beach. The winter began with a brown, lumpy desert. During the long nights and short days microorganisms beavered away diligently taking the organic compost into the clay. By late winter what had been brown and lumpy appeared tan and smooth, like a well worn carpet. In spring I now plant and sow in friable topsoil, thanks to the work of other creatures in the soil community. I dug a separate bed about twelve feet by four feet for the heritage seeds I was saving, and for other varieties kindly given to me by seed savers. I enlarged the flower beds around the house, and added a few more for catch cropping salads, marrows and cucumbers. After two summers we found that we, friends and neighbours were enjoying the vegetables so much that we needed another bed. This time I dug one on the windy southern side of the house for leeks, onions, potatoes and root crops, which will grow with the gales.

There are now several seed savers saving my Cornish spring lettuce, so I no longer do so. I save a Victorian pea, appropriately named Prince Albert. I've found it hardy, tasty, a scrambler for survival, good at over-wintering. My neighbours don't grow peas, so there is no danger of cross pollination. I return seeds to Heritage Seeds in August, saving some for another sowing. Heritage Seeds more than recompense with the seeds they give us. We've grown the current favourite of seed savers, 'Crimson Flowered Broad Bean', which enhances the brightest of flower beds. We give some seed to neighbours, sometimes flat dwellers, with small gardens. We harvest the pods when ripe and cut the plants at ground level where the root nodules return nitrogen to soil. We've also enjoyed unusual lettuce and radish varieties, potatoes, tomatoes, runner beans of pastel even bi-colour blossoms, and rare varieties of kale and garlic. The Yellow Ripple Currant tomato, sweet, tiny, yellow fruit on a spreading plant, beats into ripening even my Red Alert tomatoes, which I grew outside in Yorkshire, and still grow for a July and August crop of sweet tomatoes. Occasionally we discover why a variety became scarce: perhaps because it's a light cropper, or of indifferent taste, or has a short shelf life. Old varieties are worth preserving for genetic diversity, and simply because they contribute to what Chesterton called 'the uproarious labour by which all things live'.

Next to the pond, beneath our neighbour's ancient oak, holly and cherry plums, I left rough a few metres for wildlife. I added only some wild flowers and a bramble. At first I 'let be' the area in the hope that it would recolonize from the boundary hedge. It has provided shelter for frogs from the pond and an occasional thrush, both of whom pull their weight by gobbling slugs and snails. No hedgehog or slow-worm has yet moved in. After a year I had to interfere because dock was taking over. So I dug some out, letting other plants thrive. Nettles are especially welcome because they feed ladybird larvae with early aphids. They provide food for a great variety of insects which in turn feed birds, and they are also a habitat for the caterpillars of Small Tortoiseshell, Red Admiral and Peacock butterflies. They accelerate compost, adding nitrogen. Mixed with comfrey and water, they provide an organic tonic for the cucumber family. Part of organic growing is encouraging friendly predators which limit aggressors, such as slugs and aphids, which tear at vegetables and fruit. Nettles host some of these friends.

In addition to felling every leylandii in sight, I removed some asphalt, cement and slabs letting life live where the soil community had been smothered with the black kiss of death. A craftsman friend gave me a wedge with a hard tip and taught me how to remove concrete around walls with a sledge and club hammer. I filled the holes with top soil and humus. At Thornbank we inherited a large west facing patio. I removed some slabs in the centre. It is now a patio alive with fruit. We decided not to introduce a fruit cage, green house or polytunnel. But we do use three frames and fleece for early crops and for cucumbers. The advantage is that frames and fleece can be stored inside in winter leaving the garden open and *au naturel*. The disadvantage is that we do not have the benefits of a cage, greenhouse or tunnel. Compromise again!

Silver apples

One of the perks of Bexhill life, different but comparable to the fell walks of Yorkshire, is the proximity to the national fruit collection at Brogdale, near Faversham, in Kent. We visit Brogdale often, especially for blossom and plum walks and apple weekends where we can select apples from literally hundreds of varieties. I purchased most of my own trees from Scotts Nursery, Merriott, Somerset, and Deacons, Isle of Wight. Some very rare apple varieties I had grafted in March and July at Brogdale. Brogdale also sent me, as a 'Friend of Brogdale', red, white and pink currants surplus to the requirements of the national currant collection. I planted about eighty-five fruit varieties amounting to about a hundred plants including raspberries. By training fruit, grown on dwarfing root stock, against walls and fences one can plant a large variety even in an average garden. I planted twenty apples, especially Sussex and Irish varieties, and a few which are very rare. Among the latter is a Nonpareil, sometimes called the Jesuit apple, because according to legend, probably apocryphal, Jesuits smuggled it into England in the sixteenth century during the Allen-Parsons era. I also grow a Fall Russet from the national collection which originated in my native Detroit, and a Golden Pippin once ordered by George Washington for his orchard at Mount Vernon where, far from home, it did not thrive. I planted an Ecklinville Seedling, developed by a gardener named Logan on my ancient family estate in Armagh. Ecklinville was a popular cooker during Victorian and Edwardian times, but then faded because it is unsuitable for lorry travel and shelf life. Needless to say it is still delicious. I planted an old Irish gardener named Sam Young next to Tom Putt, an eighteenth-century Dorset vicar: ecumenism in the garden. I also grow what is reputed to be 'the ugliest apple in the world', Knobby Russet from Midhurst near here, a delicious eater which has irregular bumps on its skin. Housewives recoil, so it is another delicious rarity. My *malus sylvestris* is reportedly the one native British apple which has contributed genes to domestic apples which, like most fruit, are heavily indebted to Asia. The apple offers many graces – promise, bud, blossom, fruitlet, fruit, colour, fragrance, companionship, inspiration, even love. 'My heart is like an apple tree,' wrote Christina Rossetti.

I planted seven pears, four of them cordons on the east (front) wall. They get morning sun, little wind, and blossom when insects are stirring. Pears join daffodils welcoming spring with blossoms like quiet white bells. I planted nine plums, three damsons and a Shepherd's bullace. Six gage-like plums I trained on the south wall and fence. The other three plums, like the damson, do their best in the wind. Two of the damsons, the *malus sylvestris*, and a Nancy cherry plum, serve as an edible windbreak against the sharp east winds. Cherry plums on dwarf root stock should be planted everywhere in cities. They are wind and aphid resistant, and give fruit in July and August. One of the finest collections of cherry plums I know is that of the Benedictine Sisters of Minster Abbey. Kilnered and preserved they feed the sisters and the retreatants and guests throughout the year. The abbey goats appreciate their August windfalls.

I planted a Nabella cherry on a north facing fence near the holly tree. The latter feeds birds in winter, breaks southwest winds and provides green at Christmas, the only time I prune it. I planted an Alfred apricot in a south facing position on the fence, opposite the shade tolerant cherry. In front I planted a Dutch medlar, dwarfed by a hawthorn root stock, a beautiful tree with white blossoms and russet fruit which, when bletted, or left to become over-ripe, in the kitchen in November, makes a delicious custard-like desert. I planted, mostly on walls and fences, about fourteen currants of different varieties, two Worcesterberries, (the one soft fruit which ignores wind), an Invicta disease resistant gooseberry which gives us about eight pounds of fruit in July, a Jostaberry, two blueberries, two chaeonomeles quince, and over twenty soft fruit of the rasp-berry and blackberry tribes in addition to alpine strawberries and three rhubarb. We keep bay and myrtle bushes in con-tainers, a touch of the holy land on the patio. Barbara fastens labels and descriptions on the fruit, providing information for visitors and refreshing our own memories about details. These are much appreciated when we open the garden annually each summer for a church charity. Some people spend an hour or more studying the labels.

Fruiting commences with the Invicta gooseberry and a King's Acre berry in June. Thereafter we are virtually self sufficient in fresh fruit until October. There are of course bumper and lean spells. Soft fruit literally cascades in, some-times two pickings a day, in July. One week the boysenberry is in spate, another the tayberry, or raspberries. And during the lulls there is always the rhubarb to stretch deserts. For three weeks, beginning usually during Wimbledon fortnight (late June), we are awash with currants, red, white and pink. Barbara kilners blackcurrants, gooseberries, Worcesterberries, plums, and a varied mixture of berries. A few packets disappear into the freezer to surface in winter as mousses and sorbets and pavlova toppings. Rumpots, like humans and pekes, love apricots, but don't get any of our rare Alfreds which taste unlike any bought apricot. A homegrown apricot, like a peke, is a rare and unique thing. We store keeper apples including some from the only fruit tree I salvaged from the previous garden, a Bramley on East Malling dwarf stock. I visited the original Bramley in Southwell where it survives happily, admired by assorted visitors including scientists from universities all over the world. The present owner kindly showed us the tree and gave us a bag of apples from 'the original'. We shared them with Betty and Edwin Le Grice, former Dean of Ripon whose daughter, Cate Mack, runs a beautiful rare breeds farm with an organic shop at Norton St Philip's, near Bath. When Edwin died we asked Cate to plant there a commemorative tree. She chose a walnut.

A local gardener, Barbara's nephew Ralph, cuts our grass. Gradually we will need more help. Grass will again cover the beds. The next person who digs the garden will find more humus in the soil than I did. In my eco-theological dotage I hope to totter along the fruit trees reaching through the glistening air, with William Butler Yeats, to 'pluck till time and times are done the silver apples of the moon, the golden apples of the sun.'

Eco-theology in Bexhill

Barbara returned to her former church St Peter's in the old town. She serves on the national steering committee of Christian Ecology Link, specializing in producing that ecumenical group's informative leaflets. I worship at St Martha's, the Catholic church in this part of Bexhill. We looked around to discern where we could assist the local community, while still engaged further afield. We started an ecumenical theology evening in our lounge which meets quarterly. We distribute a paper for discussion about two months before we meet. Numbers quickly grew until we are about thirty, including some clergy and RE teachers, which is about the maximum number for a discussion group. People with a special interest sometimes suggest an article for discussion, then chair, or act as resource persons, during the meeting. We are an open ecumenical group with Anglicans in the majority.

We sponsor a Sussex 'Creation In Autumn', two autumn Monday evenings with lectures, discussions and stalls, including Traidcraft, UNA, Christian Ecology Link, and local organic produce. St Peter's community centre in the Old Town makes an excellent venue. But I see advantages to 'going on the road' some autumns, taking the evenings to other towns and even villages on the marsh. When such 'small scale' events, to borrow John Papworth's favourite phrase, influence worship, preaching, chapels, circuits and dioceses, Christian ministry and mission to God's earth will widen and deepen. If we 'only connect' the Church with the earth the prospects for the survival of both will brighten.

Many Sussex children are battery reared, driven to and from school hermetically sealed from the outdoors, escorted from home computer to 'information technology' and back, taken on tarmac to tarmac holidays, sometimes to CenterParcs, Euro-Disney or golf courses with discos. We both realize – perhaps it's the lifelong educator within – that a pressing challenge to our culture is that of relating children to their habitats and to Holy Mystery within and beyond the mountains. Children who pass our garden barely know what a pear tree is, let alone that, like a green miracle, pearlets will swell upon it. We invite passing children to familiarise themselves with the fruit, the pond and with Bertha. Some remark that the tadpoles and water boatmen are their first live ones. They've seen them on screens but never so real and personable. Some children stay an hour or more, others, instantly bored, prefer, like their parents, to regard food as beginning on shelves.

With the assistance of both local headmasters we established prize-day awards at both secondary schools, one a state comprehensive, one a Catholic voluntary aided, for relating religion and the earth. The state school's award is called 'Religion and Caring for the Earth', the Catholic school's 'Caring for God's Creation'. At first both heads – and staff – said they had an environment award, and an RE award, but did not know that religion and the environment were related. Now the prizes are part of school cultures. Ecology is integrated into both RE curricula. Each autumn we present to winners at both schools a book, book tokens, and a year's membership in Highwoods Preservation Society. I also write a congratulatory letter to the winning pupil and notify the local paper. St Richard's, the Catholic school, has added a personal trophy for prize winners. We are challenged, as is every generation, to re-interpret Christ for an ever changing today, or better, for tomorrow when we will have disappeared. The living memory of Christ is present in our world through us who transmit what we have received. The living tradition resides in all God's people and not just a few leaders. As Newman said, 'the ears of the common people are holier than are the hearts of priests.' I am still invited, as in Yorkshire, to give an occasional school assembly. Children are God's people now and of tomorrow. Their formation is worth our time. In my garden I sow seeds in spring for summer and autumn harvest. In awakening youngsters to the presence of God in the earth we plant for an already which is also not yet.

I lecture to a spectrum of people ranging from housebound prayer groups and coffee mornings, to theological conferences, rural deaneries, UNAs and university international societies. I think that small, local, even neighbourhood groups are as important as the large. I have lectured on the continent, including southern Spain, but I no longer lecture beyond northern Europe because of the 'over the top' damage jet travel does. When I meet Americans at conferences I find their perspectives not as refreshing as they once seemed. More useful would be creative – and sustainable – bioregional theologies, something academics have yet to provide.

I attend, learn from – and occasionally address – environmental, gardening and green conferences. Eco-theology includes the HDRA AGM, potato weekends at Ryton Gardens, celebrations of the tomato at Chichester, Soil Association events, Irish Seed Savers, the Green Party, meetings of SERA (the Labour sympathizers green group), Forum for the Future, CPRE, and local conservation groups. I often find more common ground, certainly more earth concern, with seed savers than I do with theologians, and certainly with jetting theologians. The Church of England Doctrinal Commission notes, 'Much of the history of theology has been characterized by forgetting as well as by learning, with the result that instead of an accumulation of knowledge and understanding we see only the replacement of one partial insight by another equally partial.' For a theologian, to help earth caring people to recover insights almost forgotten, even buried in the tradition, keeps feet on the ground, it keeps us humble: humus and humility are of the same root.

Harvest

At baptism Christ touches us in water – and water is rare and precious, sacred and luminous for the rest of our lives. Christians are people respectful of water. Jesus comes, as St John said, 'not with the water only but with the water and the blood' (1 Jn. 5.6). An Irish priest told me he always returns sacramental water to the earth because his mother so taught him. His mother, listening to her mother, heard the Mystery in the mountain where all springs begin. The peaks on the summit point to Holy Mystery within the mountain. We Christians are people of the water, and of the bread and wine, whose God became an earthling like unto us save sin. The plenitude of the Incarnation, the earthiness of Jesus the Jew, has been almost a silent doctrine. There has been in Newman's words, 'an economic relinquishment of a sacred doctrine.' The moment is now come to recover the earthiness of Jesus and of ourselves who are one with him. People of water, bread and wine, rising in Jesus who is an earthling, should be present wherever people love the earth. A spirituality of water and blood, bread and wine, of the Incarnate God who in himself contains the universe, is already an earth spirituality. Even without a human presence and spirituality, the rest of the earth community grows grain and grapes. I have seen wild cereals glistening in wind and sun in Galilee, and wild grapes scramble over fields in Michigan. Without us gaia 'can do' and does a lot. For millennia she glorified God in our absence, 'since the first sequoia forests lifted their spires to the sky,' said John Muir. *With* our presence, however, that wild beauty becomes biodiverse fields of grain and grapes brought to an intensity in bread and wine which earth has given, and human hands have made. In Christ we earthlings point gaia to God.

The shortest way home, as Chesterton said, is to go all the way around the world. I am a long way from northwest Detroit on the edge of the Michigan fields and lakes. Yet I am also back where I started, for the earth community is the same as when I opened eyes upon its beauty a lifetime ago in Michigan. It still points beyond itself to Mystery, as Hopkins said, to 'yonder, yonder, yonder'. Each autumn as I cut away fruited wood and tie in new shoots, the hope of another spring is already on its way in the quiet buds. I add humus to the soil around the trees. The trees, the soil, the humus, the whole beautiful earth shares our destiny. The point of being at home on earth, home on the range, is to leave the world, distilled in one's work and one's own garden, as good and hopefully a little better than we found it. That way the grass by being green will praise God. And the saints will rejoice in the beauty of the earth.

Notes

Chapter One (pp. 1–18)

1. Ellen Leonard, *Unresting Transformation: The Theology and Spirituality of Maude Petre* (Lanham: University Press of America, 1991), p. 4.

2. Barbara Ward and Rene Dubos, *Only One Earth* (Harmondsworth: Penguin, 1972), p. 26.

Chapter Two (pp. 19–36)

1. Gabriel Daly, 'Making Sense of Where We Are', *Religious Life Review* (January/February 1998), p. 27.

2. Walter Kaspar, *The God of Jesus Christ* (London: SCM, 1984), p. 157.

3. Sean McDonagh, 'Resolving the Third World Debt Crisis', *Eco-Theology* (July 1998/January 1999), p. 107.

4. Bruno Scott James, ed. & trans., *The Letters of St Bernard of Clairvaux* (Stroud: Sutton Publishing, 1998), p. 156.

5. John P. Galvin, 'From the Humanity of Christ to the Jesus of History: A Paradigm Shift in Catholic Christology', *Theological Studies*, (June 1994), p. 270.

6. Raymond E. Brown, *An Introduction to the New Testament* (New York: Doubleday, 1997), p. 202.

7. 'On the Diatessaron', in Sebastian Brock, *The Luminous Eye* (Kalamazoo: Cistercian Publications, 1992), p. 166.

8. His Holiness Pope John Paul II, *Crossing the Threshold of Hope* (London: Jonathan Cape, 1994), p. 44; cf. Sr. Ancilla Dent, ed., *Ecology and Faith: The Writings of Pope John Paul II* (Berkhamsted: Arthur James, 1997), pp. 34-5.

Chapter Three (pp. 37–52)

1. Pierre Teilhard de Chardin, *Letters From Hastings 1908–1912* (New York: Herder & Herder, 1965), pp. 170–71.

2. Carl Jung, *Answer to Job* (London: Ark Publications, 1984), p. 87.

3. Elizabeth Johnson, 'The Cosmos: An Astonishing Image of God', *Origins* (September, 1996), p. 206.

4. Pierre Teilhard de Chardin, *The Heart of the Matter* (London: Collins, 1978), p. 25.

Chapter Four (pp. 53–70)

1. John P. Meier, *A Marginal Jew* (4 vols.) (London: Doubleday, 1994), Vol. I, p. 253.

2. Ibid., p. 31; cf. Joseph A. Fitzmyer, *Scripture and Christology: A Statement of the Biblical Commission with a Commentary* (London: Geoffrey Chapman, 1986), pp. 65–6.

3. James Carney, ed., *The Poems of Blathmac, Son of Cu Brettan*, (Dublin: Irish Texts Society, 1966), pp. 65–7.

4. Raymond A. Brown, *An Introduction to New Testament Christology* (London: Geoffrey Chapman, 1994), pp. 236–7.

5. G. K. Chesterton, *Criticisms and Appreciations of the Works of Charles Dickens* (London: Dent, 1933), pp. 51–2.

6. N. T. Wright, *The New Testament and the People of God* (London: SPCK, 1992), p. 153.

7. W. H. Auden, 'Friday's Child' in Edward Mendelson, ed., *Selected Poems*, (London: Faber & Faber, 1979), p. 238.

Chapter Five (pp. 71-86)

1. Richard Bauckham, 'Jesus and Animals I: What Did He Teach?' in Andrew Linzey and Dorothy Yamamoto, eds., *Animals on the Agenda*, (London: SCM, 1998), p. 39.

2. Robert Louis Wilken, 'In Dominico Eloquio: Learning the Lord's Style of Language', *Communio* (Winter 1997), p. 865.

3. Raymond A. Brown, *An Introduction to the New Testament* (New York: Doubleday, 1997), p. 43.

4. Lynn White, Jr., 'The Historical Roots of Our Ecological Crisis', *Science*, 155 (1967), pp. 1203-7.

5. Cf. James Barr, 'Man and Nature: The Ecological Controversy and the Old Testament', *Bulletin of the John Rylands Library*, 55, (Manchester, 1972), pp. 9-32; Robert Murray, *The Cosmic Covenant* (London: Sheed & Ward, 1992), pp. 161-3.

6. Norbert Lohfink, *Great Themes from the Old Testament* (Edinburgh: T. & T. Clark, 1982), p. 175.

Chapter Six (pp. 87-102)

1. Manlio Simonetti, *Biblical Interpretation in the Early Church* (Edinburgh: T. & T. Clark, 1994), p. 1.

2. Richard Bauckham, 'Jesus and the Wild Animals (Mark 1.13): A Christological Image for an Ecological Age', in J. B. Green and M. Turner, eds., *Jesus of Nazareth Lord and Christ* (Grand Rapids: Eerdmans, 1994), p. 3.

3. Noel Dermot O'Donoghue, *The Mountain Behind the Mountain* (Edinburgh: T. & T. Clark, 1994), p. 23.

4. Pope John Paul II, 'Address to Youth, Rimini, 1982', *The Pope Teaches* (London: Catholic Truth Society, 1989), p. 748.

5. Quoted in Kilian McDonnell, 'Jesus' Baptism in the Jordan', *Theological Studies* (June, 1995), p. 217.

6. Gordon Lathrop, *Holy Things: A Liturgical Theology* (Minneapolis: Fortress, 1993), pp. 91-2.

7. Alan Gear, 'Comment', *HDRA News* (Summer 1995), p. 2.

8. Edward P. Echlin, *The Deacon and Creation* (London: Church Union, 1992), esp. pp. 12-18; cf. also E. P. Echlin, *The Deacon in the Church* (New York: Alba House, 1971), pp. 135-6.

Chapter Seven (pp. 103–15)

1. Steven J. Dick, *Plurality of Worlds, the Extraterrestrial Life Debate from Democritus to Kant* (Cambridge: CUP, 1982), p. 89.

2. Blaise Pascal, *Pensées*, A. J. Krailsheimer, ed. & trans. (London: Penguin, 1995), p. 60.

3. In Steven J. Dick, *Plurality of Worlds, the Extraterrestrial Life Debate from Democritus to Kant* (Cambridge: CUP, 1982), pp. 94–5.

4. Michael Crowe, *The Extraterrestrial Life Debate 1750-1900* (Cambridge: CUP, 1986), p. 558.

5. Henry David Thoreau, *Walden and Civil Disobedience*, Owen Thomas, ed. (New York: Harper, 1966), p. 89.

6. Loren Eiseley, *The Immense Journey* (New York: Harper, 1957), p. 162.

7. C. F. D. Moule, *The Origin of Christology* (Cambridge: CUP, 1977), p. 143.

8. 'Christ in the Universe' in *The Poems of Alice Meynell* (New York: Harper, 1923), p. 92.

9. Gerard Manley Hopkins, 'As kingfishers catch fire', in W. H. Gardner, ed., *Gerard Manley Hopkins: A Selection of his Poems and Prose*, (London: Penguin, 1963), p. 51.

Chapter Eight (pp. 116–34)

1. Philip Sherrard, *Human Image: World Image. The Death and Resurrection of Sacred Cosmology* (Ipswich: Golgonooza Press, 1992), p. 1.

2. Al Gore, *Earth in the Balance* (London: Earthscan Publications, 1992), p. 11.

3. Max Oelschlaeger, *Caring for Creation: An Ecumenical Approach to the Environmental Crisis* (London: Yale University Press, 1994), p. 57.

4. Ibid., p. 54.

5. Teilhard de Chardin, *Hymn to the Universe*, Simon Bartholomew, ed. and trans. (New York: Harper and Rowe, 1965), pp. 68–9.

6. Sean McDonagh, 'Saving the Seas', *Doctrine and Life* (November, 1998), pp. 557-8.

7. The World Commission on Environment and Development, *Our Common Future* (Oxford: Oxford University Press, 1987), p. 8.

8. Dick Richardson, 'The Politics of Sustainable Development', in Susan Baker, Maria Kousis, Dick Richardson and Stephen Young, eds., *The Politics of Sustainable Development: Theory, Policy and Practice within the European Union* (London: Routledge, 1997), p. 43.

9. Ibid., pp. 12-18; Edward P. Echlin, 'From Development to Sufficiency', *Fourth World Review*, Nos. 83 & 84 (1997), pp. 27-9; cf. also Paul Ekins, 'From Consumption to Satisfaction', *Resurgence*, (November/December 1998), pp. 16–17.

10. Edward Goldsmith, Unpublished Address, The Religious Education and Environment Programme (See 'Some Useful Resources' for address), (London: REEP, 1998).

Chapter Nine (pp. 135–61)

1. Beth Burrows, 'Where Nothing is Sacred', in P. S. Ramakrishnan, K. G. Saxena & U. M. Chandrashekara, eds., *Conserving the Sacred for Biodiversity Management* (New Delhi: Oxford & IBH Publishing Co. Pvt. Ltd., 1998), p. 87.

2. For the problems of air transport and travel see J. W. Rogerson, 'Reflections on Air Travel', *Eco-Theology* (July 1998/January 1999), pp. 61-7; cf. also John Whitelegg, 'Flying Off Course', *New Ground*, 52 (1997), p. 24.

Seeds for Discussion

These small seeds are for solitary prayer and thought, or for group prayer and discussion – or for both. The questions help us to concentrate our contemplation. God speaks to us, and we to God, through the Scripture texts and the texts from our living tradition.

1. **Why are there people on earth?**

· Was not the earth better before the arrival of humanity?
· Will the earth community not be better off after people disappear?
· What, in brief, is God's will for each of us while we live?

Genesis 1.26–8.
Psalm 8.
Psalm 98.4–9.
Psalm 104, especially verses 14–23.
Psalm 148.
Hebrews 2.5–9.

> We are made in a wondrous way with great glory from the dust of the earth and so intertwined with the strengths of the rest of creation that we can never be separated from them.
>
> – HILDEGARD OF BINGEN

Consider how God dwells in creatures, in the elements giving them being, in the plants giving them growth, in animals giving them feeling, and in men giving them understanding, and so in me giving me being, life, feeling, and causing me to understand; making likewise of me a temple, since I am created to the likeness and image of his divine majesty; and then reflecting on myself.

– Ignatius Loyola, 'Contemplation for Obtaining Love'
– *The Spiritual Exercises*

Earth Spirituality: Jesus at the Centre, pp. 43–7.

2. How can God, in Jesus, be an earthling?

God's Word, or Wisdom, is the immanent God's wise engagement with his creation.

· What do we mean when we say God is in Jesus?
· Can Jesus, our Creator, be an earthling like us?
· Is the cross included in earth spirituality?
· How do the gospels show the complete earthiness of Jesus?

Proverbs 8.22–31.
John 1.1, 3, 14.
1 Corinthians 1.19–24.
Luke 2.1–14.
Mark 1.13.
Luke 21.37–8.

It is Thou who makes the sun bright, together with the ice;
  it is Thou who createst the rivers and the salmon all along the river.
That the nut-tree should be flowering, O Christ, it is a rare craft;
  through Thy skill too comes the kernel, Thou fair ear of our wheat.
Though the children of Eve ill deserve the bird-flocks and the salmon,
  it was the Immortal One on the cross who made both salmon
                                                    and birds.
It is He who makes the flower of the sloes grow through the surface
  of the blackthorn, and the nut-flower on other trees;
Beside this, what miracle is greater?

                                        – 'Christ's Bounties',
                                        CELTIC PRAYER

        Whatever was the form and expression which was given
        to the clay (by the creator), Christ one day to become
        man, was in his thoughts.

                                        – TERTULLIAN

Earth Spirituality: Jesus at the Centre, pp. 61–70.

3. How can we live earth spirituality with Jesus?

· We can share spirituality with people, but with God?
· Is not earth spirituality about people, as the voice of the earth, relating to God?
· Does Jesus' closeness to the natural world bring him closer to us?
· How important for us is Nazareth?

· Did he learn spirituality from Mary his mother?
· Can we pray with him in the community of Mary and the other saints?

Mark 1.35.
Luke 2.39–40.
Matthew 6.7–14.
Luke 22.39–46.
John 19.25–7.

Heavenly Father
your Holy Spirit
gives breath to all living things;
renew us by this same Spirit
that we may learn to respect
what you have given
and care for what you have made
through Jesus Christ
your Son, our Lord.

Almighty God
your Son, Jesus Christ,
taught us to love
even the least among us,
give us the courage to care
for all living creatures
and the strength to defend
even the weakest of all.

– From the RSPCA Order of Service

The King looked up, and what he saw
  Was a great light like death,
For Our Lady stood on the standards rent,
As lonely and as innocent
As when between white walls she went
  And the lilies of Nazareth.

– G. K. CHESTERTON
'The Ballad of the White Horse'

Earth Spirituality: Jesus at the Centre, pp. 54–7.

4. What about earth spirituality in church?

· How can we include the earth in church?
· Is perhaps earth spirituality a personal spirituality that has nothing to do with 'the church'?
· How can the church, as listening community, be earth spiritual?
· Are the sacraments and rites of passage earth spirituality?
· Is not the feast of Christ the King, at the threshold of Advent, a great earth spiritual feast?

Matthew 26.26–9.
Luke 22.17–19.
1 Corinthians 11.23–6.
Acts 2.42–7.
Revelation 5.13.

We have to do it — just the two of us — just you and me. There is no 'them' — there is nobody else. Just you and me. On our infirm shoulders we must take up this heavy burden *now* — the task of restoring the health, the wholeness, the beauty and the integrity of our planet. We must start the Age of Healing now! Tomorrow will be too late.

— JOHN SEYMOUR

Since trees and plant life, as a whole, have an indispensable function with regard to the balance of nature, so necessary to life in all its stages, it is a matter of ever greater importance for mankind that they be protected and respected. For the Christian there is a moral commitment to care for the earth so that it may produce fruit and become a dwelling of the universal human family.

— POPE JOHN PAUL II

The whole creation
was altered by thy Passion;
for all things suffered
with thee,
knowing, O Lord,
that thou holdest all things
in unity.

— *From the Byzantine Rite*

Earth Spirituality: Jesus at the Centre, pp. 94–102.

5. What about the future of the earth?

- Are not humans destroying the earth?
- After humans disappear – or self-destruct – will not the earth sizzle or fade into nothingness?
- What does it matter to believers whether the earth has a future or not?
- Does not salvation through Christ mean that our souls will leave our bodies and the earth?
- Does heaven include the earth?

Genesis 9.9–10.
Habakkuk 3.17–19.
Romans 8.19–25.
Ephesians 1.1–10.
Revelation 21.1–4.

> There is no salvation without the participation of creation, no redemption that by-passes the world, no heaven without earth. Christian salvation is never purely a spiritual affair, never simply a mystical union with God, never just anonymous absorption into the divine. The resurrection of Jesus from the dead affirms that the individual whole person and material creation are directly involved in the coming-to-be of God's final gift of salvation.
>
> – DERMOT LANE

For those, O Lord,
the humble beasts
that bear with us
the burden and heat of the day,
and offer their guileless lives
for the well-being of humankind;
and for the wild creatures, whom Thou hast made
wise, strong, and beautiful,
we supplicate for them
Thy great tenderness of heart,
for Thou hast promised to save
both man and beast,
and great is Thy loving kindness,
O Master,
Saviour of the world.

— ST BASIL THE GREAT

Earth Spirituality: Jesus at the Centre, pp. 128–34; 160–61.

Some Useful Resources

Organizations

Agriculture Christian Fellowship, Thorpe End Cottage, West Thorpe, Willoughby-on-the-Wolds, Loughborough LE12 6TD.

ASWA (Anglican Society for the Welfare of Animals), PO Box 7193, Hook RG27 8G.

Brogdale Horticultural Trust, Brogdale Road, Faversham, Kent ME1 8XZ.

Centre Naturopa, Environment, Conservation and Management Division, Council of Europe, f-67075 Strasbourg Cedex.

Christian Ecology Link, 20 Carlton Road, Harrogate, North Yorkshire HG2 8DD.

Christian Socialist Movement, Westminster Central Hall, London SW1H 9NH.

Church and Conservation Project, Arthur Rank Centre, Stoneleigh, Warwickshire CV8 2LZ.

Compassion in World Farming, 5A Charles Street, Petersfield, Hampshire GU32 3EH.

CPRE (Council for the Protection of Rural England), 25 Buckingham Palace Road, London SW1W 0PP.

CRUC (Christian Rural Concern), Manor Farm, Warmington, Banbury OX17 1JL.

CSCAW (Catholic Study Circle for Animal Welfare), 12 Swan Court, Whitney, Oxon OX8 7EA.

EcoCongregation, ENCAMS, Elizabeth House, The Pier, Wigan WN3 4EX.

ETA (Environmental Transport Association), 10 Church Street, Weybridge, Surrey KT13 8RS.

European Christian Environmental Network, c/o Conference of European Churches, PO Box 2100, CH-1211, Geneva 2, Switzerland.

Forum for the Future, 9 Imperial Square, Cheltenham, Gloucestershire GL50 1QB.

Friends of the Earth, 26/28 Underwood Street, London N1 7JQ.

Friends of the Royal Botanic Gardens, Kew, Richmond, Surrey TW9 3AB.

Fruit Nurseries:

> Deacons Nursery, Godshill, Isle of Wight PO38 3HW.

> F. V. Roger, The Nursery, Pickering, North Yorkshire YO18 7HG.

> Scotts Nursery, Merriott, Somerset TA16 5PL.

Green Democrats, 72 Cumnor Hill, Oxford OX2 9HU.

Green Party, 1A Waterlow Road, London N19 5NJ.

Greenpeace, Canonbury Villas, London N1 2PN.

HDRA (Henry Doubleday Research Association), Ryton Organic Gardens, Coventry CV8 3LG.

ICOREC (The International Consultancy On Religion, Education and Culture), 3 Wynnstay Grove, Fallowfield, Manchester M14 6XG.

Irish Seed Savers, Capparoe, Scariff, Co. Clare, Eire.

John Muir Trust, 41 Commercial Street, Leith, Edinburgh EH6 6JD.

John Ray Initiative, TC103, Francis Close Hall, Cheltenham & Gloucester College of Higher Education, Swindon Road, Cheltenham GL50 4AZ.

Lifestyle, 78 Filton Grove, Horfield, Bristol BS7 0AL.

Network of Christian Peace Organizations, c/o 21 Cuckoo Hill Road, Pinner, Hertfordshire HA5 1AS.

Pax Christi, Christian Peace Education Centre, St Joseph's Watford Way, Hendon, London NW4 4TY.

RSNC (Royal Society for Nature Conservation), The Green, Witham Park, Waterside South, Lincolnshire LN5 7JR.

SERA (The Socialist Environment and Resources Association), 11 Goodwin Street, London N4 3HQ.

Society, Religion and Technology Project, 45 High Street, Edinburgh EH1 1SR.

Soil Association, Bristol House, 40-56 Victoria Street, Bristol, Avon BS1 6BY.

Spiritearth, 148 Robbins Road, Arlington, MA 02476-7528, USA.

Traidcraft, Kingsway, Gateshead, Tyne & Wear NE11 ONE.

Transport 2000, The Impact Centre, 12-18 Hoxton Street, London N1 6NG.

UNA (United Nations Association), 3 Whitehall Court, London SW1A 2EL.

VOICE of Irish Concern for the Environment, 7 Upper Camden Street, Dublin 2, Eire.

WEN (Womens Environmental Network), PO Box 30626, London E1 1TZ.

Publications

Baker, S., Kousis, M., Richardson, D. and Young, S., eds., *The Politics of Sustainable Development* (London: Routledge, 1997).

Brock, Sebastian, *The Luminous Eye* (Kalamazoo: Cistercian Publications, 1992).

Catholic Bishops' Conference of England and Wales, *The Call of Creation: God's Invitation and the Human Response* (London: Catholic Communications Service, 2002).

Clark, Stephen R. L., *Animals and their Moral Standing* (London: Routledge, 1997).

Dent, Sr. Ancilla, ed., *Ecology and Faith: The Writings of Pope John Paul II* (Berkhamsted: Arthur James, 1997).

Eaton, John, *The Circle of Creation: Animals in the Light of the Bible* (London: SCM Press, 1995).

Echlin, Edward P., *The Deacon and Creation* (London: Church Union, 1992).

Edwards, Denis, *Jesus the Wisdom of God: An Ecological Theology* (New York: Orbis, 1995).

Guroian, Vigen, *Inheriting Paradise, Meditations on Gardening* (London: Darton, Longman & Todd, 2001).

Harvey, Graham, *The Killing of the Countryside* (London: Vintage, 1998).

Lane, Dermot, *Keeping Hope Alive* (Dublin: Gill & Macmillan, 1996).

Matthews, Anne, *Wild Nights, the nature of New York City* (London: Flamingo, 2001).

Mayne, Michael, *This Sunrise of Wonder* (London: Fount, 1995).

Mooney, Christopher, *Theology and Scientific Knowledge: Changing Models of God's Presence in the World* (South Bend: University of Notre Dame Press, 1997).

Muir, John, *His Life and Letters and Other Writings*, Terry Gifford, ed. (London: Baton Wicks, 1996).

O'Donoghue, Noel Dermot, *The Mountain Behind the Mountain: Aspects of the Celtic Tradition* (Edinburgh: T. & T. Clark, 1993).

Oelschlaeger, Max, *Caring for Creation: An Ecumenical Approach to the Environmental Crisis* (London:Yale University, 1994).

Seymour, John, *The Complete Book of Self-Sufficiency* (London: Dorling Kindersley, 1997).

Sorrell, Roger, *St Francis of Assisi and Nature: Tradition and Innovation in Western Christian Attitudes Toward the Environment* (Oxford: OUP, 1988).

Wright, N.T., *The Challenge of Jesus* (London: SPCK, 2000).

Index